Local History

Local History

A Handbook for Beginners

Philip Riden

MERTON PRIORY PRESS

First published 1983
by B.T. Batsford Ltd

Second edition, fully revised, 1998
Reprinted 2000, 2011

Published by Merton Priory Press Ltd
9 Owen Falls Avenue
Chesterfield S41 0FR

© Text Philip Riden 1983, 1998
© Cover illustration Award Photography 1998

ISBN 978 1 898937 27 2

Printed by Dinefwr Press, Llandybie,
Carmarthenshire SA18 3YD

Contents

The Public Record Office
and other National Collections, *continued*

Preface

As the first chapter explains in more detail, this is a fully revised second edition of a book I originally wrote in 1982, based partly on my experience of teaching local history in adult education since the mid 1970s and partly on my own enthusiasm for the subject over a rather longer period. The first edition, published in 1983, was reissued with minor corrections in 1989 and remained in print until the early 1990s. Since then I have been trying to find the time to make the extensive revisions needed to bring the information contained in it up to date, so as to be able to publish a new edition that would be of genuine value as a practical manual for both adult students and undergraduates, and perhaps also older pupils in secondary schools (or at least their teachers).

Not only has the text been thoroughly overhauled, notably to take account of the extensive changes in the location of records, both nationally and locally, but I have also revised and extended the reading lists to each chapter. This has been at the expense of including any illustrations in the text, since otherwise the book would have been lengthened (and thus the price increased) in a way which I wished to avoid. It has in fact been possible to publish this new edition at a lower recommended retail price than the last printing of the first edition nearly ten years ago.

I am very grateful to a number of colleagues (in particular Dr Julia Bush) for suggesting that this book was worth updating and reissuing, to Brian James and my wife Elizabeth for help with proof-reading, and to Anne-Marie Knowles of Chesterfield Museum & Art Gallery for help in choosing an illustration for the cover.

Nene University College   Philip Riden
Northampton
September 1998

CHAPTER ONE

Local History
Yesterday and Today

Aim and approach

The aim of this revised edition of a book first published in 1983 remains the same as it was fifteen years ago: to provide a simple introduction to the study of local history in England and Wales. It is intended mainly for two types of reader. The first are part-time amateur enthusiasts with no previous experience of historical research who are keen to discover something of the past around them. Such people have probably never been as numerous as they are today, as is evident from the support for local history groups up and down the country, the popularity of evening classes, and the demand for the services of county record offices and local studies libraries. This vigorous amateur interest is paralleled by the popularity of the subject in schools, colleges and universities, especially for dissertations, and it is to students in these institutions that this book is also directed.

The modern growth of interest in local history has brought with it an upsurge in publication, ranging from substantial academic monographs through the mass of books and pamphlets published by individual local historians or societies, to the ephemeral newsletters of such groups, as well as the more scholarly annual volumes of the older antiquarian societies. A distinctive element in this literature has been a succession of books on how to study local history, or some aspect of the subject. The pioneer of this sort of work was W.G. Hoskins, who from the late 1940s was popularising the 'Leicester School' of local history in articles, broadcasts and later books, culminating in the first edition of his classic introductory text, *Local History in England* (1959). Others at work in the same period produced not merely many excellent examples of the 'new local history' of communities in which they were interested, but also 'how to do it' books or occasionally 'why do it'. Several other introductory textbooks followed, as well as guides to particular topics, some of which, such as family history, industrial archaeology, vernacular architecture and landscape studies, now have a substantial literature of their own.

In 1973 W.B. Stephens's *Sources for English Local History* provided a more detailed general guide to both primary and secondary source material than any previous book of its kind; last revised in 1981, Stephens remains useful as a technical manual, although it is inevitably beginning to go out of date. In 1987 my own *Record Sources for Local History* attempted a somewhat fuller, and rather differently arranged, guide to archival material.

Neither Stephens's *Sources* nor my *Record Sources* could be described as a book intended for beginners, nor is either particularly readable. Indeed, my main reason for writing the first edition of the book reissued here was a belief, based on several years' experience of teaching local history in adult education, that there was scope for a straightforward, up-to-date introductory text, which sought to survey the whole field of local history in England and Wales and tried to provide practical guidance for those wishing to embark on their own studies. The book was generally well reviewed and appeared to retain its value with my own extramural students for another decade or more, even though it was gradually becoming out of date. Since my recent return to undergraduate teaching, I have been pleasantly surprised to discover that the book has also proved useful in this field.

It is certainly true that since 1983 no-one has attempted another book on similar lines with any success; the only more recent general survey which can seriously be recommended to either undergraduates or adult students, Kate Tiller's *English Local History. An Introduction* (1992), is not only conceived on a much larger scale but is organised in a different way. Among more discursive work, David Hey's attempts to show that family history and local history are more closely related than the practitioners of either tend to believe are well worth reading, while his various 'Companions' to both subjects are by far the best of this type of encyclopaedia-style compilation. Two recent books should be treated with caution. Michael A. Williams's *Researching Local History* (1996) can perhaps best be described as stimulating, but despite its title is not a practical guide. By contrast, *Exploring Local History* by James Griffin and Tim Lomas (1997), published in the generally reputable 'Teach Yourself' series, attempts to be exactly this with disappointing results. Some of the advice offered is misleading (and occasionally simply wrong), while the standard of English is depressingly low.

Like the original edition, whose basic structure it retains, this new version of my own book has been written in the belief that there is still scope for a short handbook on 'how to get started' in local history, not how to write the definitive community history or a higher degree thesis. It has been written against a background of my own interest in local history—largely untutored—since my early teens; twenty years' experience of teaching adult classes as a full-time tutor in a university extramural department which in its heyday had a large and varied local history programme; and, most recently, the rather different experience of teaching undergraduates while at the same time working as a county editor for the Victoria County History. Whatever its faults, the book can at least claim to be based on practical first-hand experience: in my present job I divide my time, on the one hand, between teaching local history to undergraduates (including supervising short dissertations) and leading an adult research group and, on the other, between working daily either in a county record office or at the Public Record Office. I also retain my long-standing involvement with the organisation of local history as general editor of one of the country's larger county record societies.

My recent career change partly explains why the emphasis in the new edition has moved somewhat away from regarding extramural students as the main readership, as was the case in 1983, since I now realise (or at least hope) that the book has some value for undergraduate courses, especially those assessed by dissertation. Equally, it also reflects the relative decline of extramural work as one of the main driving forces in the growth of local history, as was certainly the case from, say, the late 1950s until the 1980s. The diminished role of the extramural tutor is itself partly a consequence of declining numbers (a decline which will continue over the next ten years as remaining staff retire, with no serious prospect of replacement) and the fact that amateur local history has matured. The subject can now stand on its own feet, without sponsorship from extramural departments, which in any case are no longer able to provide the support they once did.

In the chapters that follow the reader will find a clear, up-to-date guide to basic sources for local history, plus hints as to where to find out more. Each chapter has a list of further reading (pp. 177-90). There is now an enormous literature on particular sources, which, together with the more general references, should lead the reader beyond the deliberately modest limits of this book. What this book should do, however, is provide a grounding in what local history is about and how it is studied.

Most, if not all, general books on local history are arranged in one of two ways. Either the information is set within a broadly chronological framework, as in my own *Record Sources* or Kate Tiller's *Introduction*, or it is arranged by topic, so that one has chapters on local government, education, religion and so on. Both approaches have their merits, particularly in books which go into more detail than this one. But neither is necessarily the most accessible for the beginner. Such people may be interested in only one aspect of their community, or in some theme not amenable to study within a parish (such as industrial archaeology or family history). If they are interested in their town or village as a whole they will soon be overwhelmed by what is available and wish to narrow down their interest to one topic—such as the development of transport, or the community as viewed through the enumerators' books of a single census. The other possibility is that their interest will widen out from a very narrow starting point—most commonly the history of their own family or their house, or perhaps a single industrial enterprise.

Whatever the starting point, one thing is certain. Most newcomers will not, as some of the weightier manuals suggest they should, take a topic (say transport in a local community) and start working through all the secondary literature (which in this case is huge, and will require the resources of a big city library, if not a university). Even more certainly, they will not work systematically through the primary sources for their chosen subject, wherever they may be (for transport history much material is held in London which the amateur living in the provinces can usually only visit occasionally). They will instead go to their local library, look at what is available in the reference department on transport history, and then go to the local studies section to see what there is on the immediate locality. The next step will be to go to the county record office, in the hope of finding more from local archive material. Only after working in this way for some time will most amateurs go to the Public Record Office or one of the other central repositories, or follow up obscure printed references in a copyright library or a major academic or public library. Beginners want to be told how they can make worthwhile discoveries quickly from what is available to hand, not given a long list of widely scattered archival source or a lengthy bibliography of printed material, much of which can only be found in a few libraries.

Similarly, most do not need the thoroughness of some of the published work on particular records. For example, while almost all local historians use maps, few use quarter session records, which feature in all the textbooks but are some of the least produced documents in county record offices. Similarly, with two conspicuous exceptions (bishop's transcripts of parish registers and probate records), the non-parochial records of the Church of England are also, despite the existence of a thorough guide, little used except by academic researchers. This book does not aim to list every possible source for a particular topic, nor does it describe everything to be found in a county record office. It concentrates on subjects which amateurs tend to be interested in, and material available in local libraries and record offices which they can use without encountering great technical problems.

Another consideration is that not all parts of England and Wales offer the same scope for local history. (As in all books of this kind, Scotland is omitted, since its administrative and judicial history have created a separate system of records which cannot easily be dealt with alongside sources for England and Wales.) Most of the archival material used by local historians is the product of an administrative process, mainly at local level, and the English counties have had the same administrative arrangements since the Middle Ages. Wales was shired by Henry VIII and since then the Welsh counties have been subject to the same legislation (with a few exceptions) as those in England. Similarly, the local administrative history of the Church of England (including until 1920 the four Welsh dioceses) has been uniform for a long time. What is sometimes not made clear is that different parts of the country have vastly dissimilar histories of archive preservation, even if archive creation originally took a similar form everywhere. In general, the southern English counties have the best preserved records, those of the north and west, and even more so Wales, the least. Discoveries of this kind can be disappointing to a beginner, who has identified what should be available from a textbook and seeks out such material in a local record office. For example, the everyday lives of yeoman farmers in Tudor Devon cannot, despite what some books may say, be recreated from that county's share of the thousands of probate inventories that survive in every county record office: most of the Exeter probate records were destroyed during the Second World War. This problem is most acute in Wales, where whole tracts of early modern material simply do not survive, and where local history is frankly often a frustrating experience before about 1750. As one who until recently had done all his local history in a either a northern (or at least north midland) county or Wales, I have tried to be more realistic than some earlier writers whose experience seemed to be drawn only from a richly endowed Home Counties record office.

A similar problem often exists with the material in record offices that has been deposited privately. It is not always made clear that the existence of a manor does not necessarily mean that the record office will have court rolls from 1300 to 1925, while most guides to sources notoriously exaggerate the survival of business records (businessmen have always been far too busy to keep proper records, or to be interested in preserving them; some industries, e.g. coal, have had a positive interest in destroying archives). Similarly, the vagaries of landownership have not always produced the tons of estate material which local record offices have for certain major families. A great deal may have been burnt when a mansion was pulled down in 1920, or when it was requisitioned by the Army in 1939. Likewise, despite the impression given in some quarters, solicitors earn a living by acting for clients, not devoting time and space to the preservation of old papers until the record office seeks to take them on deposit. Some old established firms never make deposits, some have nothing to deposit because it was all destroyed in a fire two years ago.

These observations may bring comfort to archivists worn down by explaining that their holdings do not correspond in every particular with what it says in a general guide; they may seem depressing to intending local historians. They should not worry unduly, since they will almost certainly be able to discover something about the topic they are interested in. But common sense should tell them that some county councils are more generous than others in how many staff they provide for their record office, or how large a search-room or strong-rooms. Some offices have been in existence for much longer than others; not only have they had more time to collect records but, equally important, they have had longer to list and index them. The same is true of local studies libraries, which vary greatly in the richness of their holdings and the service they offer the public.

The evolution of local history

Although the present approach to local history owes much to the work of W.G. Hoskins and others in the years immediately after the Second World War, as developed and refined by many people since, the subject itself is much older. Hoskins and his contemporaries grew up during a particularly sterile period in English local history—the years between the two World Wars—in which there was little innovation and the institutions which had served antiquaries before 1914 were in decline, with nothing to replace them. The new teaching and research at Leicester and elsewhere took local history out of the doldrums and sent it in exciting new directions. But looking back there was another golden age, between about 1870 and 1914. And so it goes on, with periods of vitality interspersed with periods of quiescence or stagnation, back to the beginning of antiquarianism, which is one small facet of the reception of the Renaissance in England in the second half of the sixteenth century.

Today's local historians owe more than they are sometimes willing to admit to the long history of their own subject, especially the buoyant periods of that history. In the first place, there is a legacy of local topographical writing—the secondary published sources with which virtually all research begins—which can best be understood in the context of the development of the subject. Coupled with this is an archival legacy of 'antiquarian papers', compiled by past local historians, containing extracts from records, notes on churches, and descriptions of field monuments. This material is sometimes ignored by present-day investigators, but it is important as part of the 'history of local history' (more broadly, the history of ideas) and can often be a valuable source. A third reason why local historians should know something about the evolution of their subject is that much of the institutional framework within which the subject is organised is best explained historically. Why, for example, should a body with the eminently reasonable name of 'British Association for Local History' have been founded only in 1982?

While the study of History in the widest sense is one of the oldest pursuits of civilisation, the same is not true of what we now know as local history. Looking simply at England, it is fair to say that most medieval people were not interested in topography. Contemporary chronicles obviously mention localities associated with political or military events, and some form a source for the history of the places in which they were written. But people did not travel up and down the country for pleasure, nor, for the most part, did they draw maps and plans. With a few exceptions medieval historians did not search archives for local source material, nor write descriptions of where they lived.

The influence of the new learning in Elizabethan England led to the complete rewriting of English political history for the first time since the twelfth century; men also became interested in local history. This interest took two main directions. On the one hand were those anti-quaries, most often lawyers or men who had spent some time at an Inn of Court, who searched the archives of central government for refer-ences to their own county, starting with Domesday Book (1086), the oldest public record which has been continuously in official custody, and proceeding through later material, all of it heavily biased towards the history of landownership and the descent of manors. Parallel with this interest arose a fascination for genealogy which, with ups and downs, has lasted to the present day. The great promoters of sixteenth-century family history were the heralds, who in the course of their perambulations around the country (the Visitations) noted not merely the pedigrees of landed families but also heraldic glass in church and manor house windows and church monuments with heraldic decora-tion. As in later ages, the professional heralds were imitated by amateur enthusiasts. Thus, at the same time as peerage families were beginning to send their sons on the 'Grand Tour' of southern Europe to view the newly rediscovered splendours of Greece and Rome, the gentry, with their more modest but nonetheless broadening horizons, were looking for the first time at their 'country', meaning the county in which they had their estate, in which they were justices of the peace, and which was the focus of their political, economic and social life.

By the 1570s this interest in genealogy and topography was beginning to bear fruit in published work. The earliest 'county history' (in reality as much description as history in the usual sense) was William Lambarde's *Kent* (1576), written by a lawyer and, not surprisingly, devoted to one of the Home Counties. Before the end of the century works had been published for several other counties and much more had been collected but not published. The first half of the seventeenth century saw further developments until in 1656 the herald and future Garter King of Arms William Dugdale published his *Warwickshire*. This marked the climax of pre-Restoration local history and was imitated a good deal after 1660, for example in Robert Thoroton's *Nottinghamshire* of 1677.

Dugdale's *Warwickshire*, in its format and content, epitomised the first century of English antiquarianism. In the first place it was the work of a gentleman. The landed gentry or gentry-lawyers practically monopolised this era of antiquarian writing: the antiquary-cleric of eighteenth-century caricatures belongs to a later period. Secondly, it was divided into two parts of unequal length. The book began with a general description of its chosen county, its geology and natural history, administrative geography, markets and fairs, rivers and hills, and 'political history' from the Anglo-Saxon heptarchy to the present. Having summarised the essential features of the county as a whole, the author proceeded to describe each parish within it, either in alphabetical order or, more likely, with the parishes arranged by 'Hundred', the ancient subdivision of a county in southern England, known in the East Midlands and North as a 'Wapentake'. The account of each parish would be taken up very largely by two topics: the manor and its owners since 1086 and the church and its contents, especially monuments. The more ambitious county history might introduce other material, either in the general section or under the appropriate parish: discoveries of prehistoric or Roman antiquities, charitable benefactions, interesting natural phenomena. The more legally minded the author, the more emphasis there would be on manorial history; if he was more interested in heraldry, church monuments and topography, there would be a bias in that direction. Overall, however, the scope of the early county history was limited and for this reason has little appeal to modern local historians.

The first generation of county histories is significant partly as a reflection of educated men's vision of their locality in the sixteenth and seventeenth centuries: their view of the county as the natural unit about which to write, even though they did not normally use county records; their emphasis on the manor and manorial tenures, sometimes to the exclusion of lesser landowning families in a parish; and their more or less careful recording of church monuments, with domestic architecture, including even manor houses, often wholly ignored. Secondly, the books are important because they determined the mould in which local history would be written down to 1914 and even beyond: the division of the county into parishes and manors; the division of the history into 'general' and 'parochial' sections. But they are still useful today, especially the more ambitious seventeenth-century compilations. Despite their old fashioned arrangement and content, the county histories often provide the most thorough account of the history of a manor and of the families that owned it. There is far more to village history today than the descent of the manor, but in many parts of the country the manor remained an important local institution until the nineteenth century, and to know who was the main landowner in a parish is the obvious starting point in any search for manorial or estate records. Similarly, the description of the church may seem irrelevant, but the building could have been entirely altered by the Victorians, leaving a seventeenth-century account as the only guide to what it looked like when the men and women listed in the first parish register were baptised, married and buried there. For someone interested in nineteenth-century brickmaking there will not be much in the traditional county history, but those interested in the community as a whole should not deride the stately volumes in which these histories were usually published, even if their authors' views of the local community were very different from ours.

By the middle of the eighteenth century, histories had appeared for most English counties. The period 1660-1730 was one of great scholar-ship in English history and this was reflected in local topography, as some of the 'Friends of Clio' who formed the readership for the new history tried their hand at writing. The half-century after 1730 was less productive but between about 1780 and 1830 there was a new upsurge of interest, partly on familiar lines, but in other ways breaking new ground. Several of the older histories were reissued, usually with 'Additions' claiming to bring them up to date: thus Thoroton's *Notting-hamshire* reappeared in 1790 in three volumes instead of one. Counties of which no previous account had been published were described for the first time but still in an entirely traditional manner: Theophilus Jones's *Brecknockshire* (1805-9) is a remarkable example of this in a poor, thinly populated Welsh county. Leicester, for which William Burton provided a brief history as early as 1622, practically sank under the endeavours of the antiquarian publisher John Nichols.

What was new in English antiquarianism during the first generation of its 'Romantic' phase was the emergence of the travel account as a distinct branch of topographical writing. There are a few well known earlier travel diaries, such as those of Celia Fiennes or Daniel Defoe, but the great growth of such literature dates from after 1750, and especially the half-century before the coming of the railway virtually killed the genre. Some of these books are purely descriptive; some, such as Arthur Young's tours, have a specialist interest in improvements in farming. Others, such as William Bray's *Sketch of a Tour into Derbyshire and Yorkshire* (1782), are solidly antiquarian and provide, often with numerous engraved plates, descriptions not merely of churches but also of medieval domestic buildings, archaeological discoveries and much else. Works of this kind are invariably worth checking in case the tourist mentions the place you are interested in, and early tours may provide the first reference anywhere to archaeological features then being uncovered. Tour literature must be treated with some caution: some accounts are fictitious and merely describe journeys around their authors' library of similar works; rather more are based on genuine tours but reiterate what previous visitors said about much visited places (e.g. Bath or the Wonders of the Peak), adding nothing new.

The tour diary spawned a more local literature of guidebooks about particular places or guides to country houses, then being increasingly visited by the new tourists; it also had some influence on the writing of county history. More topographical description and more field archaeology crept in alongside the pedigrees and arms; ruins of religious houses and castles were described as well as the church. The first phase in the history of archaeology as a separate discipline also belongs to this period and is reflected not only in tours and county histories but in new journals, of which *Archaeologia*, published by the Society of Antiquaries of London, was the most important. The beginning of the nineteenth century saw a spate of short-lived journals rivalling both *Archaeologia* and the *Gentleman's Magazine* as outlets for antiquarian writing, most of which were not, like their successors later in the century, produced by societies but by the same commercial publishers who were producing the county histories, tour books and collections of prints of the same period.

Finally, it is worth mentioning—especially for readers in counties lying alphabetically between Bedford and Devon—the most ambitious project of these years, *Magna Britannia*, an attempt to produce uniform histories of every English county. Daniel and Samuel Lysons, one a record keeper in the Tower of London, the other a Cotswold parson, were not the first to conceive this scheme and certainly not the last. As early as 1586 William Camden had actually produced, in a single volume, a description of every county in Britain. His *Britannia*, first published in Latin, was enlarged and ultimately translated several times before his death in 1623, and then reappeared, yet further enlarged, on the crest of each wave of later antiquarian enthusiasm. Thus it was edited by Edmund Gibson, future Bishop of London, and a team of local correspondents in 1695; a century later the dilettante collector Richard Gough (1735-1809) produced a new edition in 1789, superseded by a three-volume folio recension, also edited by Gough, in 1806. Each edition contained more on individual manors and families, but even the last could not match the Lysonses' ambition to write a standard, if fairly brief, county history for everywhere from Bedfordshire to Yorkshire. Their books conform to the established pattern, with 'general' introductions followed by parochial histories. The series, which never came near completion, is probably most useful for counties such as Derbyshire which have never had a 'classic' history by a local author.

After the efflorescence of antiquarianism in the period 1780-1830, which produced a vast and by no means wholly original literature, the next turning-point came in the middle decades of the nineteenth century with the building of the railways, the emergence of an educated middle class, the mechanisation of printing, and another intellectual revolution comparable to that of the sixteenth century.

All these developments profoundly changed the way in which local history (including field archaeology) was pursued. As well as destroying a great deal, the railways led, directly or indirectly, to the discovery of much archaeology. Cuttings sliced through prehistoric ditches and banks and exposed accumulations of worked flint; the lines that followed carried people in greater numbers than before and at less expense on excursions to visit those monuments which were not obliterated. The people who went on these excursions were not so much the gentry who had hitherto written most local history, or the individual travellers who described their journeys in the earlier diaries. They were the clergy and the new professional classes created by the Industrial Revolution, especially architects, who contributed much to the careful recording of medieval buildings, as well as over-restoring village churches. These people were far more numerous than the eighteenth-century antiquaries and more gregarious. Above all, they joined societies: the second half of the nineteenth century saw the creation of most of the English county antiquarian societies which have since bulked so large in the promotion of local history, archaeology and, at least in the past, natural history.

Welsh county societies, it may be added, are mostly twentieth-century foundations, although the Cambrian Archaeological Association, covering the whole of Wales, is much older.

The archetypal county society of the later nineteenth century had its headquarters in the county town, where it would either rent rooms or, if it was lucky, acquire a convenient castle, as at Lewes or Taunton. The lord lieutenant would usually be its president, and the diocesan bishop and other resident peers a bench of vice-presidents. The membership at large would be a combination of gentry, professional people and clergy. The society's aims would generally embrace natural history as well as archaeology and local history; its activities would include lectures and excursions, the publication of an annual report and transactions, the formation of a library and museum, and possibly also the appointment of a 'vigilance committee' to warn clergy against excessive church restoration. The growth of a new middle class created the membership of such societies; a long era of cheap printing that was to last up to 1914 enabled them to publish on a scale that few have been able to since.

The most enduring monuments to the county societies are their journals, which in most counties constitute, from around the 1860s, a vast store of articles, long and short, good and bad, which are always worth searching for any large-scale community history today. Amid the derivative descriptions of churches and manor houses visited by the society the previous summer, and the lepidoptera report for 1891, will be found otherwise unpublished discoveries, transcripts of medieval charters now lost, and pedigrees of families on which no modern work has been done. As with the county history, the traditional county journal has little to say in its earlier numbers about, say, Victorian brickmaking, but for the village historian it remains a major source.

The period which saw the birth of most of the county societies was not such a productive age for the county history. A few societies made early attempts to produce collaborative volumes, but in general there was a realisation that the explosion of historical knowledge in the nineteenth century had at once rendered most county histories out of date and made their replacement or even revision by a single author virtually impossible. This revolution in historical research stemmed partly from an early nineteenth-century concern for the preservation of Britain's immensely rich heritage of public records, evinced by the appointment of a succession of royal commissions from about 1800, and the establishment in 1838 of the Public Record Office as a home for millions of documents scattered between a variety of unsuitable repositories in different parts of London. Although little was done in this period for local records (except enquiries by the Record Commission about borough and quarter sessions records and John Rickman's attempts to abstract population data from parish registers), the creation of the PRO was a great stimulus to historical research and to the publication of transcripts or catalogues of the main classes of medieval administrative records. Ultimately, this led to a revolution in the way in which English history was written; at local level antiquaries could now re-examine many of the documents used by their seventeenth-century predecessors. As more material was published, first by the Record Commission, then by the Master of the Rolls (the titular head of the PRO), then by a growing number of national and local societies, so the printed sources for local history, even the narrowly conceived history of manorial descents, multiplied. As the nineteenth century wore on, a similar process led to the opening up of ecclesiastical archives for the first time and the publication of collections of medieval deeds (especially the cartularies of religious houses), all of which swelled the available material for a county history.

As local antiquaries abandoned ambitions to write county histories, so they became more concerned with individual parishes. In a sense, this reflected the changed social circumstances of the authors. Whereas a seventeenth-century gentleman saw the county as his natural frame of reference, a late nineteenth-century parson naturally settled for an account of the parish in which he had the cure of souls. Between about 1870 and 1914 dozens of parish histories were published, some as long as an early county history, others no more than enlarged church guides. Hundreds of smaller scale endeavours ended up in local journals. To help these new authors one of the most active, if not always most careful, of clerical antiquaries, John Charles Cox (1843-1919), produced a modest manual entitled *How to Write the History of a Parish* (1879), the first modern local history textbook. Although originally intended as an aid to the compilation of a collaborative history of Lincolnshire (which proved abortive), Cox's book was most widely used by those seeking merely to write a history of their own community; its scope amply demonstrates what was expected of the thorough parish historian of the day.

The climax of this Victorian heyday of antiquarianism, marked by so much new publication and by a much wider interest in the subject, came in 1899 with the launching of a project to equip every county in England (but not Wales) with a new history, still conceived on traditional lines but executed with a uniformity and thoroughness that even the Lysonses never dreamt of. Instead of two men covering the whole of the county there was to be a team producing uniform chapters, first for a series of 'general' volumes and then for another of 'topographical' volumes, containing parish histories. When it was completed, the scheme would enable the reader to turn up an authoritative history of any parish in England, or a definitive account of the Roman remains, schools, religious houses or whatever (including natural history) of every county. The project was also designed to yield a substantial profit to its promoters, who secured royal approval to call it the 'Victoria History of the Counties of England'. Her Majesty lived to see only one volume of VCH published, but the following two hundred and more have all been dedicated to her memory.

Like the county journal, VCH is often among the first sources which beginners come across in their local library. For most counties, at least two volumes were published before the First World War, usually completing the 'general' articles envisaged in the original plan; only for about a dozen counties were the parish histories all published, generally by the 1920s. The early volumes normally provide the best available text of Domesday Book for the county (with introduction, translation and map), and useful if brief accounts of religious houses and the older schools. The archaeological articles are obviously out of date and the chapters on political and economic history are very general, although the sections on individual industries can sometimes still be valuable as a starting point. Like the county journals, VCH may seem old fashioned but is still worth consulting, and in counties where it is active today the far more detailed topographical volumes published since the 1950s are invaluable.

The story of the Victoria County History is very much a microcosm of how English local history has developed since 1900. Initially, rapid progress was made with the new series, until a financial crisis struck in 1908, which had not been solved when the outbreak of war in 1914 brought the project to an almost immediate halt. After 1918 the society which had supported so much antiquarian endeavour was greatly reduced in numbers and wealth; subscribers for schemes of all kind, VCH included, were much harder to find. The number of counties for

which the History continued to be published fell; other publishing
ventures ceased altogether. The county journals generally survived,
although annual issues grew thinner. There was also an intellectual
stagnation. Little was written that was new in approach: in most
counties books and articles remained cast in a traditional mould and
tackled traditional topics. There were no new projects for county
histories outside the VCH scheme, except in some Welsh counties
where substantial public subsidies were secured.

Local history today

As in so many fields, it was only at the end of the Second World War
that a real revival in local history began. It took many forms, one of
which, the work of W.G. Hoskins and his supporters at University
College, Leicester, where a Department of English Local History was
established in 1948, has already been mentioned. His *Local History in
England* (1959) was highly influential in deciding how the subject was
studied at all levels. Parallel with this new academic impetus, of which
the revival of VCH in several counties was another aspect, came the
establishment of a Standing Conference for Local History under the
aegis of the National Council of Social Service. This was a federation
of county committees, themselves made up of the new groups then
springing up in towns and villages all over the country. Whereas the
county societies, at least in England, are now mostly over a century
old, the smaller groups which most local historians join first have
rarely been in existence for more than forty years and often much less.
Lacking the conservatism and what some would see as the pretensions
of the county societies, these new groups were the spearhead of post-
war amateur enthusiasm for local history. As they became established,
their newsletters evolved into magazines, lecture meetings developed
into group research projects, and many societies worked towards the
publication of a collaborative town or village history.
    A further important post-war stimulus to research was a great
expansion of teaching by university extramural departments and other
providers of adult education. Much of this remained traditional in that
the audience simply listened to lectures, but some tutors led research
groups which studied communities in depth, taking advantage of the
capacity for a coordinated group of students to digest voluminous and

possibly repetitive records much more quickly than could an individual on his own. V.H.T. Skipp has described work of this kind which he was pioneering in the West Midlands in the early 1950s; by the 1970s it had become a standard and very popular feature of most extramural programmes.

Research projects of this kind, whether by individuals or groups, led by societies or classes, would have been impossible had it not been for the establishment of a record office in virtually every county and a number of boroughs in the decade after 1945. Those offices which had been set up in the 1920s and 1930s enlarged their holdings, both of administrative records and private deposits, especially estate papers, as there was a further round of country house sales after the Second World War. The increased resources of record offices, coupled with the coming of cheap photocopying, greatly widened the scope for research from original documents housed other than in distant and inaccessible London repositories.

Under the influence of scholars such as Hoskins and his successor at Leicester, H.P.R. Finberg, local historians since 1945 have studied a subject transformed out of all recognition since its last period of popularity at the end of the nineteenth century. The emphasis is now on the community as a whole: the landless as well as the landed; the poor as well as the rich; the Nonconformist chapel as well as the parish church; trade and industry as well as farming; working class suburbs and council estates as well as pleasant countryside and pretty villages. At the same time, the chronological scope has widened: local historians now pursue the early history of motor-car ownership as well as the history of coaching inns; the impact of the slump of the 1930s as well as the plague of the sixteenth century. Topography itself has enjoyed a new vogue as 'landscape history'. The study of past industry, using field evidence as well as documents, has been popular since the 1960s as 'industrial archaeology'. The memories of elderly residents are sought not, as used to be the case, for recollections of local customs or folk songs, but to capture on tape some idea of what domestic service was like before the Second World War. All this is local history of one kind or another, and much of it, especially where the integration of visual and written evidence is concerned, has a longer history than some of its present practitioners realise.

One other renaissance should also be mentioned, although it owes nothing to the Leicester School. This is the quite phenomenal popularity enjoyed over the last twenty years by genealogy, which has a long tradition but which in its new guise of 'family history' has attracted thousands of new enthusiasts, led to the establishment of dozens of new societies, and placed considerable pressure on local record offices. The rate of growth of interest has perhaps now levelled off, although the numbers involved remain very large, and it is possible (which was not the case when this book was first published) to see that this enthusiasm has had some wider benefits. Some family history societies have done excellent work indexing bulky source material (notably the census enumerators' books); the huge market provided by family historians has made possible the publication of a whole series of specialised guides to records; and many of those who start using record offices to trace their own ancestors find that their interests broaden out into wider aspects of local studies.

The modern expansion of local history has created a correspondingly vast literature of newsletters, booklets and journal articles. In most counties there is now a more popular magazine alongside the traditional county journal, offering an outlet for more modest pieces of research. Groups, individuals, record offices and libraries publish booklets embodying the results of research, or describing particular sources. There are also two general magazines devoted to the subject. The newer and perhaps livelier title is *Local History Magazine*, which is published commercially and has a strong bias towards news, reviews of new publications and listings of local society activities, as well as some longer 'how to do it' articles. *The Local Historian* was also founded as a private venture (as *The Amateur Historian*), as long ago as the early 1950s, but for most of its life has been published by the Standing Conference for Local History or its successor, the British Association for Local History. *TLH*, which is issued to members together with a news magazine, has more academic main articles and more critical revIews.

Unlike the old Standing Conference, the BALH offers membership to individuals and is the only national voluntary body catering for local history as a whole, although the Historical Association, one of the oldest subject teaching organisations, has traditionally done a good deal to promote local studies. In addition, there are numerous more specialised national groups, such as the Society for Landscape Studies, the Vernacular Architecture Group or the Association for Industrial Archaeology, as well as the network of local, national and special interest family history societies, for which the Federation of Family History Societies acts an umbrella organisation. Gregarious local historians have the choice in most counties of joining a traditional county society, which may on closer inspection prove less stuffy and pretentious than at first sight, or a smaller group in their own town or village. This may also be stuffy and pretentious, or it may do no more than hold lectures and excursions; more likely, however, is that it will contain a nucleus of keen members engaged in their own research or combining in a group project. It may publish a newsletter and possibly research papers; the county society will have a journal and probably other publications.

Alternatively (or in addition), the would-be amateur researcher can join an evening class, which will probably provide an opportunity to look at, if not actually work on, photocopies of documents. Many universities and colleges (including the Open University) also offer part-time courses leading to a diploma or certificate in local history, and several have part-time M.A. courses in the subject (or in more general historical studies, including an opportunity to do some local work). All such courses, at whatever level, usually require the preparation of a short dissertation based on original research.

I will merely conclude, as I did in the opening chapter of the first edition, by suggesting that before embarking on any course of this sort, or even joining a society, the prospective local historian might do worse than read the rest of this book.

CHAPTER TWO

At the Library

The local studies library

People become interested in local history for many different reasons and their approach will vary accordingly. Someone investigating the comparatively recent past may well start by talking to older residents and not look at documents, maps or books at all. Others, especially those interested in genealogy or the history of their house, may have some of the source material—for example, birth certificates or deeds—in their own possession. In general, however, most local historians, sooner rather than later, realise that their local library or record office is likely to have much of what they want and will accordingly present themselves at one or the other. Some researchers, with some idea of what they are doing and possibly in search of a specific type of record, will go at once to the record office. Absolute beginners, or those with an interest in their community as a whole, will do much better to start with the resources of the local library and then investigate the record office.

In principle, local studies libraries collect books, periodicals, pamphlets, maps, illustrations, printed ephemera and, in recent years, audio and video recordings relating to their area, while record offices are concerned with the archives of the authority which provides the service and with documents entrusted to their care by others. The division between libraries having printed secondary sources and record offices having primary manuscript material is not absolute—some libraries have large manuscript collections and all record offices have some printed books—but this is roughly how the material is arranged.

Free public libraries in England and Wales are well over a century old and today provide a wide variety of services. The collection of local material is one of their older functions. It was the municipal authorities who first established libraries, the county councils following only after the First World War, and it was the boroughs that built up the largest local collections. Sometimes these were very comprehensive: the magnificent city libraries of Sheffield and Birmingham, for example, have traditionally collected material relating to north Derbyshire and south Staffordshire respectively, not merely their own authority's area. This sort of coverage is a legacy of the days when there was no public library service outside the boroughs and it was natural for a library in a county town to take in books and other material for the whole of the shire or adjoining region. After 1945 the county services built up collections but, given the scarcity even then of so much of the older material found in a local studies library, they were unable to collect retrospectively to rival the holdings of longer established libraries.

This historical background is useful in understanding how local studies collections are arranged, because the distinction between borough and county holdings, outside the former metropolitan counties, was blurred by local government reorganisation in 1974. After this date, except for four special cases in South Wales, non-metropolitan district councils ceased to provide library services, and so throughout the shire counties the older borough libraries became part of an enlarged county service. This transformed county libraries' holdings of local material and allowed many to think for the first time in terms of a coordinated service throughout their area. Sadly, progress of this sort has been dealt a severe, and possibly fatal, blow by the further reorganisation of local government in Wales in 1996, when county councils were abolished and replaced by 22 mostly smaller all-purpose authorities, and similar piecemeal changes in England. Here a number of former county boroughs have been reborn as 'unitary authorities' and have resumed the running of their own library service, quite separate from that of the surrounding county, which continues to provide a network of branches for the smaller districts.

Even in counties in which all the libraries are still administered by a single authority, it is important to appreciate that a former county borough library is likely to have some unique material for its immediate locality; that the main collection in the county will almost certainly have material for the whole of the area and not merely the county town; and that at least the larger of the old borough collections will be richer than a collection at the county library headquarters, even if the latter is closer to the record office and thus seems the most convenient place to work.

General comments such as these cannot fully explain the various ways in which local studies collections are organised, but local historians will soon grasp how the system works in their own area, especially as virtually all library services issue leaflets describing their local studies collections. In the larger unitary authorities, especially the former metropolitan districts, the main public library will usually have an old established collection forming its own department with at least one professionally qualified member of staff, while the smaller services may house theirs in the reference library, whose staff can only devote part of their time to local material. In rural counties there may simply be the collection in the county town; elsewhere there will probably be a network of small and medium-sized collections in the former boroughs.

Because of the wide variety of local studies libraries—large and small, well housed and cramped, well catalogued and neglected, regional and local—it is difficult to explain in detail what the local historian will find in any particular area. Unless they already have some experience of using specialised libraries, most readers will feel overwhelmed on their first visit to a large city library and so it is probably best to start with a smaller borough library. All such libraries should have many of the printed sources outlined in the previous chapter: the classic county histories, whatever has been published of the Victoria County History, a complete run of the county journal, and much of the monograph and pamphlet literature relating to the county. This is basic stuff and local historians interested in their area as a whole, rather than a specific topic, should find plenty to be going on with in this material alone. VCH may, as explained in Chapter 1 (p. 15), be a disappointment, except for supplying a reliable text of Domesday Book and perhaps a short history of the local grammar school, but if there is an older county history that should at least provide an outline account of the manor and a description of the church.

The extent of finding-aids will depend on how long the collection has been established and what resources have been available for its development, but most local collections have a catalogue arranged by place, which should locate any published parish histories. It may also identify articles, or there may be a separately published index in the county journal itself. In some counties, the library will have a series of local record society volumes, or a series published by the society that produces the main journal. These will be volumes of edited documents relating to the county, either transcribed at length or summarised ('calendared'). Again the volumes should be indexed: if you are interested in a particular parish try searching under that name. The older volumes will be concerned mainly with medieval documents and may contain lengthy stretches of untranslated Latin, but it is worth making a note of any reference to your parish for the future, even if you do not at first grasp what exactly the reference means.

Note-making for local historians

The phrase 'making a note' raises the whole question of organising your material. Many visitors to a local studies library, or indeed a record office, have a very casual interest in what they are looking for and never pursue their enquiries after a first visit. Others do, and find that the notes they took early on in their work are so badly organised that they have to do much of it again. If you are interested in exploring the history of your parish, or some other topic, in any depth, possibly with an eye to eventual publication, it is worth taking from the start some simple steps towards organising what you do properly.

The best way to start any local history research project is to buy a large pad of lined, margined A4 file paper and a file to keep it in. This may sound banal, but it is surprising how many people still start on the back of an envelope and then cannot make sense of what they wrote a month later. If the notes were made at a library some distance from home this is money as well as time wasted. A4 file paper is greatly superior to a spiral-bound 'reporter's' pad or anything smaller, simply because the sheets can be filed. At first they will all go in one file, preferably with card dividers to separate different subjects; later you will need several. A4 paper can be moved about between files; sheets stapled together in an exercise book cannot. Similarly, card indexes soon grow to such a size that they become too bulky to cart round to libraries and record offices; the cards also have a propensity to fall out and get lost not shared by paper in a ring-file. Indexes have their use, for example for storing bibliographical references, but for ordinary note-making A4 paper remains the cheapest and simplest medium.

A half-way house between A4 file paper and small record cards, which has been standard practice for VCH since the inception of the project in 1899 but appears not to be widely used by others, is to make notes on what VCH calls 'slips', i.e. sheets of A5 paper (arranged upright, not lengthwise like a record card), putting a single piece of information on each sheet, with a note of the source and a heading (giving the place, subject and date to which the information relates)

under which the slip can then be filed. Anyone interested in using such
a system in a county where VCH is currently in progress will find the
county editor happy to explain in more detail what has proved for many
years to be a flexible and convenient note-making technique.

A significant development in both local history and genealogy in
recent years has been the widespread use of personal computers, either
alongside conventional filing systems or in their place. For most
amateur enthusiasts this means the use of a desk-top home computer,
on to which material collected conventionally at a library or record
office is later transferred, since laptop computers which can be used
directly for note-making remain relatively expensive and thus largely
the preserve of the academic historian whose employer provides the
equipment, although this may change over the next few years.

Computers are undoubtedly of considerable value in local history,
especially in database applications where they have largely superseded
card indexes (and thus been widely adopted by genealogists), and also
in preparing text for publication (see Chapter 7). On the other hand, as
the basis of a note-keeping system they have disadvantages, the chief
of which is the rate at which both hardware and software become
obsolete. A related difficulty is the limited volume of storage space on
small machines, especially at the cheaper end of the market favoured
by home computer users. In extreme cases, one may be left with data
collected only a few years before which can no longer be retrieved
because both operating systems and programs have changed; a more
common problem is the risk of loss or deterioration of the growing
number of floppy discs required to store a large collection of notes.
Difficulties of this sort will almost certainly diminish, rather than
increase, as more sophisticated equipment becomes more widely
available, but for the time being a traditional paper-based filing system
still has much to commend it.

What do you write on the paper, especially on your first visit to a
library? A sensible plan is to start by searching whatever finding-aids
are available and making a note of useful references, then to follow up
the more obvious of these, such as articles in the county journal or a
parish history. It is a good idea to keep a separate list of references and
tick them off as you look at them. Some may be so specialised that you
will not feel they are relevant, but it is worth keeping them for the
future.

The books and articles you trace are best listed in the same way as they appear on library catalogue cards or a computer-based catalogue. There is no great mystery about the accurate presentation of bibliographical references and it does make it much easier to find things later. Full details are given in Chapter 7 (pp. 165-7), alongside advice on writing footnotes, but (briefly) for a book you need the name of the author, the title and the date of publication, in that order. If you are requisitioning material from a closed-access stack you will also need the class-mark, which in most public libraries will be a locally adapted version of the Dewey decimal system. For a journal, note the author and title of the article, the name of the journal, the volume number and year of publication, and the first and last pages on which the article appears. This may sound a little complicated but it is important to know where a particular article can be found and also how substantial an item it is. Avoid the temptation just to note the title of the journal and the year: you will not remember a month later whether this was a passing reference or a complete article.

Having got some references to look at, it is equally important to make notes from each book in an organised way. As far as possible, make notes from different sources, especially if they are on different subjects, on separate sheets. This will make more elaborate subdivision of your filing system easier later. What is vital is to repeat the bibliographical references at the head of the sheet, unless it is a very basic source, in which case the author's name will probably do. A local historian working in Nottinghamshire should find 'Thoroton' a sufficient reference to the main county history, and in any county notes from VCH can be so headed, rather than treating each chapter as an article. For articles proper, however, it is important to note author, title and other details. A second basic point is to note the page from which your notes are taken. This is essential if you wish ever to publish a properly annotated article and desirable if you wish to retrace your steps in the future. The margin of A4 file paper is well adapted to accommodate page numbers.

Once into this simple discipline, you should be able to work steadily through printed material relevant to your chosen topic, making notes whose source can be identified and noting references which a librarian can find for you. A few other points should perhaps be made at this stage. One is to beware of the temptations of the coin-operated photocopier now available in all public libraries. Certainly, cheap copying has revolutionised most kinds of historical research; in particular one no longer has to trace maps laboriously. In a record office it is a useful short-cut if you want one document from an office a hundred miles away or it is going to take you an hour to struggle with a difficult hand. But in a library it is worth remembering that photocopiers do not actually read the books for you, and they certainly do not make intelligent notes on the bits that are relevant to your work. Simply to identify a dozen articles and get them all copied is not historical research, it is welcome income for the library and provides the researcher with a pile of copying that still has to be digested. Unless your opportunities to visit libraries are very limited, try to sit there and read the stuff rather than rely too heavily on a copier. If you do make copies of particular pages—say of maps and illustrations—it is best to copy them on to the same A4 size paper as your own notes, so that they can be filed together, rather than A3 sheets, which have to be folded or filed separately.

Another rather obvious point is that few, if any, public libraries lend material from the local collection because of its age and scarcity. Here it is worth investigating the book collection of the county society. Their 'library' may be just a cupboard somewhere in the public library (some are much larger) but for most counties you can still fit the basic printed sources into a cupboard and most societies allow members generous borrowing privileges. A £12 or £15 subscription may seem more reasonable if you establish what else you get for it besides a rather stodgy journal and six lectures a year at the other end of the county.

Following up leads

The library catalogue should give you a good start in any local history project, especially when coupled with advice from the staff, who in a local studies library have often been there a long time and know their collections well. Undoubtedly the simplest enquiry to answer is one about a place, especially a parish. The fundamental importance of the parish in local history will become more apparent when we look at archival sources in Chapter 3 but even for printed material it is still the unit under which information is most commonly organised in library catalogues.

Searchers after specific subjects may have to think more carefully about how best to quarry out material. For some topics, for example transport history, the catalogues should lead straight to a large local literature. For well known personalities, there should be an obituary notice if nothing else. The sort of enquiry that is harder to answer is one about an obscure subject or a minor person or building. Family historians or those interested in the history of their own house will rarely find ready made references to either their grandfather or their home in a local collection catalogue: here the best advice is probably to 'think in parishes'. There may be nothing, according to the catalogue, on the history of your mid nineteenth-century former farmhouse, but the farmers will certainly be listed in directories and the house may be mentioned in a descriptive article on the parish in which it stands. If it is of any architectural interest it will appear in the statutory list of buildings so designated, which is also arranged by parish. Likewise some Victorian worthy whose obituary fails to appear in a well indexed cuttings collection may be mentioned in a completely unindexed 300-page history of his home town published in 1901 and catalogued under the name of the place. Similar advice applies to those interested in minor industries. Nothing may have been written about basket-weaving in the county as a whole, but histories of particular parishes in which it once flourished may have snippets of information.

It will soon become clear to the local historian working in the library that, as was shown in Chapter 1, the literature of local history has been accumulating for a long time and that one writer has borrowed from another, with or without acknowledgement. Most modern work on local history, and most of the basic sources such as VCH and county journal articles, contain bibliographical references and it is from these that the beginner, having exhausted the immediate scope of the library catalogue, will move on to more obscure material. Over the last century historians have erected a mighty apparatus for identifying sources in footnotes to scholarly works; elements of this system can be traced further back in the older county histories: Much of this jargon can be off-putting, especially the bits in Latin, although in recent years there has been a welcome trend towards simplifying annotation. For un-scholarly references there is the added challenge of guessing what the author actually meant.

Leaving aside the citation of documents in record offices, which is discussed in the next chapter, references to printed works should be given in the form explained above, either within the text itself or in a footnote. Problems stem from repetitive references where the writer has used the old fashioned formula' Smith, *op. cit.*, p. 91' , rather than what is now regarded as standard modern practice, 'Smith, *Barset*, p. 91'. Both refer back to a full reference to the standard history of Barsetshire, but whereas there will only be one Smith's *History and Antiquities of the County of Barset* there may be numerous works by people called Smith cited earlier in the book. '*Op. cit.*' means the work previously cited; its cousin '*art. cit.*' means a previously cited journal reference, for which '*loc. cit.*' (the place cited) is sometimes also used. The continued use of these is not to be encouraged: it is far better to use a short title for second and subsequent references. Likewise, it is a sign of pretentiousness for modern local historians to write' *V. supra*, p. 1' when they want the reader to look back to the first page; in journals the phrase '*Ante*, xxv. 16', referring to page 16 of an article published in volume 25 of the same series, is also obsolete and a full author-title-year reference should be used instead. In the older county histories another Latin term likely to perplex the beginner is *penes*, as in 'Deed *penes* H. Smith gen.', which simply refers to a deed then in the possession of Mr Smith. What has happened to his deeds since 1750 is another problem.

Incomplete or obviously inaccurate references can often be identified by an experienced librarian, since the chances are they will be from one of the standard local histories; what may cause more difficulty are heavily abbreviated references to general published works. In VCH or a modern monograph such abbreviations will be explained in a list at the front of the book, but the author of a parish history published in 1900 would have considered it an insult to his readers' intelligence actually to have explained what '*Val. Eccl.* v. 504' meant. Most commonly, these will refer to published editions of medieval material in the Public Record Office, which tend to be available only in the larger public or university libraries. The older county histories may contain even more obscure references to earlier editions of the same texts, or to records now in the PRO but accessible in published calendars. A brief guide to this is almost impossible but in practice most beginners do not follow up references like 'Pat. 31 Ed. III m. 5d' or 'Esc. 10 Hen. VII n. 21'. If necessary either a local librarian or the staff of the PRO will translate mystifying algebra of this sort into modern usage and explain where to find it. (Both these examples in fact refer to sources of which there are straightforward published texts in English.)

Gradually, the assiduous local historian will work backwards through a jungle of references and identify archive sources to be pursued in either local or national repositories. There is still, however, much to be gleaned from library material. Leaving aside maps, to which Chapter 4 is devoted, and the manuscripts housed in some libraries (considered together with local record office collections in Chapter 3), some of the most useful printed primary or semi-archival material in a library are those outlined in the next two sections.

Directories

One basic printed primary source which all beginners soon encounter are directories, consisting of classified lists of residents in each parish with a short descriptive introduction about the place. Directories first appeared in London at the end of the seventeenth century and spread to provincial towns about a hundred years later. After various attempts from the 1780s onwards to publish a single national directory had proved largely unsuccessful, a pattern emerged by the 1850s of county directories, with a few national publishers, of which Kelly and White are the best known, and many local firms who issued a single town or county directory. The books are usually called *History, Directory and Gazetteer of Barsetshire* and follow a standard plan. There is a short introduction on the county as a whole and then an entry for each place, usually by parish. Sometimes the parishes are arranged alphabetically through the county as a whole, sometimes they are grouped by hundred, or (even less conveniently) with rural parishes clustered around market towns.

For each parish there is an introductory 'history', the strictly historical parts of which, like the general introduction, usually come straight from the main county history and are wholly unoriginal. Lists of carrying and coach services (later railways and omnibuses), foundation dates of churches and chapels, an outline of local government (useful as this becomes more complicated after 1870), and details of acreage and population are much more valuable. Even if the information is to be checked later (e.g. the date of establishment of a gas-works from its authorising Act of Parliament), directories are a reasonably reliable short-cut to start with. The actual lists of names are usually divided in nineteenth-century volumes between the 'Nobility,

Gentry and Clergy' (toned down to 'Private Residents' after the First World War) and a classified list of tradesmen, from 'Academies and Schools' to 'Wine and Spirit Merchants', often with the pubs and inns listed separately.

Towards the end of the nineteenth century the introductory 'historical' paragraphs about each place tend to become shorter and more space is devoted instead to two new features. For larger towns street directories were prepared, in which the roads were arranged in alphabetical order and each house (with the house-number or name and householder's name) listed. Second, a classified trade list for the county as a whole was included, as well as those for individual towns. Directories on these lines continued to be published for all English counties (and for South Wales and North Wales) between the two World Wars but after 1945 only appeared for a diminishing number of large towns, as Kelly's and other publishers found it impossible to compete against the classified telephone directories issued free by the Post Office. Early telephone directories, it may be noted in passing, can be exploited in much the same way as county and town directories, although few local libraries seem to have kept comprehensive collections for their area.

Classified trade lists in directories are tremendously useful. They can be used to trace the career of one person or a family through several businesses or (once houses in towns begin to be numbered) the various occupiers of a single property. In the countryside they will usually supply a succession of tenants for a particular farm. So, of course, will census enumerators' books (pp. 35-9), and more thoroughly, but directories are a quicker source of information. For the historian of a local industry, directories are much the best place to start, either for one business or for an industry over a wide area, rather than scanning maps, searching the census or (worst of all) expecting to find business records (see p. 76). For someone interested in a rural parish or a reasonably small town, a run of directories from about 1840 to the First World War provides a detailed introduction to the community's history and an admirable springboard from which to move on to more specialised sources. After 1920 directories become less useful in this respect, as particular places tend not to have classified trade lists, which instead were only printed for the county as a whole. Detailed local analysis is thus harder, although one can still use the lists to trace individuals or companies.

For a local historian, or perhaps a group, setting off on a fairly ambitious community study, a project worth considering is to take all the available directories and to make a slip index (or computer database) of every entry in every edition. The results can then sorted in at least three different ways. Arranged by trade the work will yield a fairly complete census of local industry for much of the nineteenth century, from which one can trace the rise and fall of various types of employment. Arranged topographically in a town (in which houses are numbered) it will illustrate the changing character of each street (residential to professional; professional to commercial), as well as the history of each house. Arranged by name it will provide outline biographies of tradesmen and manufacturers over two or three generations. Even before this material is linked to maps (Chapter 4) or census records (pp. 35-9), you have a good idea of what your community was like in Victorian times, down to the level of individual houses, businesses and families, which is satisfying in itself and should suggest further lines of enquiry.

Newspapers

Another basic source for nineteenth- and twentieth-century local history to be found in all local studies libraries are files of old newspapers. These are much bulkier than directories and their full exploitation is usually the work of years. The oldest provincial newspapers date from the early eighteenth century, originating as a single folded sheet, with at least two of the four pages devoted to advertisements and much of the rest consisting of reprints from the London press. The earliest papers were regional in scope and the amount of strictly local news before about 1830 is limited. The advertisements can be useful in themselves but even a prolonged search of an eighteenth-century paper for references to a small village is unlikely to be very fruitful. For the history of the town in which the paper was published it will be more worthwhile, as will a search for a specific event which you know happened within say a year of a given date. Truly local newspapers, with a circulation covering only one town, sprang up mainly after stamp duty was repealed in 1860 and from then until the 1950s, when a decline set in as costs rose faster than income, they are a mine of information. During their late nineteenth-century heyday weekly papers were truly 'journals of record', with council meetings reported in detail, speeches at opening ceremonies printed verbatim, and court proceedings given in full. For any aspect of a late Victorian town, especially crime and politics, newspapers are an inescapable source and far more informative than official records such as minute books or (even if they survive) court registers.

The disincentive to making extensive use of newspapers is simply their bulk. If available in their original form (which is no longer generally the case) they emerge from the stacks as large, rather fragile volumes, pieces of which tend to come away in the hands of even the most careful reader. If produced on microfilm, they are wearing to read for long periods, even on a large-format viewer, although if a reader-printer is available it is possible to make photocopies to study at home.

Whatever the medium, it is notoriously easy to become side-tracked in making newspaper searches and almost as easy to miss relevant items. Victorian sub-editors did not favour eye-catching headlines or helpful cross-heads halfway down the column; the usual format was a solid block of very small type, often printed from a worn font on poor paper. The best approach is probably to do a little at a time over a long period. Ask the library about indexes: some local studies departments, in more leisurely and better staffed days, had time to make subject indexes to at least their earlier holdings, which can save a great deal of time, as well as wear and tear on fragile volumes. Some evening classes have also tackled newspaper indexing projects and deposited the results in the library. Even if there are no general indexes available, a library may have indexed birth, death and marriage notices because of their genealogical interest.

Another short-cut is to ask about cuttings files. Compiling such files is also an activity for which there was more time in the past than today and, like indexing, involves a fair amount of subjectivity as to what to cut out and which file to put it in, but even so such files can be extremely useful, especially if they are indexed. A file of obituaries, for instance, or one on local railway history, may exist; other possibilities are cuttings of country house sale notices, or advertisements and news items concerning work on listed buildings.

Scrapbooks

Older local studies libraries may also have scrapbooks of printed
ephemera. As with most local studies librarianship, much depends on
the vigilance, enthusiasm and workload of previous librarians, who had
time to collect local theatre or football club programmes and put them
into guardbooks alongside production or team photographs and
possibly newspaper reviews and reports. A member of staff interested
in railways may have gone out and taken large numbers of photographs
in the early 1960s as local branch lines were closed and stations
demolished, putting them with press cuttings in a scrapbook of recent
railway history. Someone may have given the library his comprehensive
collection of local beer-mats, bottle labels and other ephemera of the
licensed trade. This 'non-book' material, as librarians warily describe it,
is not always fully catalogued but is worth asking about.

Pictures

Two other categories of material in local libraries have already been
touched on. One is the photograph collection (or, strictly speaking,
picture collection, although most of the items will be photographs)
which all old borough libraries have and which will have been
exploited mercilessly over the last twenty years for *Grandfather's
Barsetshire, Yesterday in Loamshire* and *Victorian and Edwardian
Almost Anywhere in Old Photographs*, apart from more specialised
publications. Few local historians need to be reminded of the value of
old postcards, photographs, prints and engravings which make up the
illustrations collection of local studies departments. They may be loose
in folders or mounted in albums, they may be indexed or roughly sorted
by place, they may form a full record to the present day or be strongest
for the pre-1945 period. Some will include the results of systematic co-
operation between the local camera club and the library to make sure
that buildings are recorded before demolition; occasionally one finds
the results of a similar project at the turn of the century.

Whatever the scope of the collection it is almost always worth
consulting, especially if it is indexed, and photocopiers can now produce
reasonably clear working copies of most originals. In particular, colour
photocopiers, because of their greater sensitivity to different tones of

grey, produce excellent copies of black and white originals. For publication a more expensive photographic copy will be needed, unless the original can be lent to the printer to scan direct into a typesetting file, but few things liven up a history of Calvinistic Methodism in Blaenycwm as much as a group portrait of the chapel deacons in 1932.

It is worth adding that most local museums also have photograph collections, and indeed collections of printed ephemera and other semi-archival material. Both libraries and museums always welcome donations which augment their picture collections and gifts of this sort represent a valuable way in which local historians interested in photography can repay some of the debt they owe to institutions on whose resources they depend heavily for their research.

Antiquarian collections in libraries

Most libraries (and museums) have at least some manuscripts. In some cases the material is similar to that which would now normally be directed to a local archive service and has ended up in a library by historical accident, most commonly because the library was established long before the record office (pp. 41-4). One type of manuscript source, however, which when held locally tends to be found in a library rather than a record office, is the notes of earlier antiquaries. The collections of the major seventeenth- and eighteenth-century antiquaries are generally preserved nationally, especially in the British Library Department of Manuscripts or the Bodleian Library, Oxford, as Chapter 6 explains (pp. 151-5); county record offices may have acquired some material by purchase or in family deposits. But public libraries tend to be strongest in more recent collections, which are often very local in scope but sometimes extremely useful.

Collections of this kind are an awful warning to present-day local historians of the danger of accumulating notes unsystematically or never writing anything; some are a reminder of what large houses people used to live in, in which there were box-rooms which could literally be filled with boxes of grandfather's almost completed history of Barchester. For the local historian with fairly easy access to the library it is worth ploughing through dozens of school exercise books filled with neat longhand transcripts from the county history or scrapbooks full of menus from pre-war Masonic ladies' nights, because occasionally you will come across something original. It may be an obscure but accurate bibliographical reference, or a note that a local solicitor has all the papers of a particular family or business, or a description of what was on the site of Woolworth's before 1950. Other antiquaries compiled card indexes of local biography or coats of arms or stained glass. There is always much dross in collections like this, but they are not usually very arduous to search and the results may be rewarding.

Census enumerators' books

Microfilm has already been mentioned as the means by which libraries make old newspapers available to readers. The other major class of material which local historians use on microfilm (or microfiche) are the enumerators' books from the nineteenth-century censuses, which are among the best known sources for genealogy and a mine of information about any Victorian community. Strictly speaking, enumerators' books are part of the archives of central government and the originals are kept by the Public Record Office. In practice, however, most local historians use microfilm copies of the books in their local library or record office and so they may most conveniently be described here. Since the books are relatively straightforward to use and yield large amounts of information without presenting many technical problems, they also fit into a chapter on 'how to get started', rather than one on more specialised sources.

A census has been taken in Great Britain every tenth year since 1801, except in 1941. Until 1831 the enumeration consisted merely of a count by the overseers of the poor of the number of people (male and female), houses and families in each parish or township, with a simple attempt at occupational analysis. Occasionally, lists of names turn up in parish collections in local record offices (pp. 51-4) which are a legacy of these early censuses. The establishment of the General Register Office in 1837 made it possible for the first time in 1841 to conduct a more sophisticated census, using the local officials of this department plus a large number of temporary employees, the enumerators. Since 1841 each household has been required to complete a form given out a few days earlier by the enumerator, on which must be listed the name of everyone who spent 'census night' in the house, with information about each person. In 1841 this merely included name, address, approximate age, occupation and whether or not the person was born in the same county as that in which he was then living. In 1851 the form was refined to include a column for marital status, the relationship of each person to the head of household, exact age, and parish and county of birth. The schedule of 1851 remained basically unchanged down to 1891, the last year for which the books are open to inspection. (Since they contain personal detail, the books are closed for a hundred years, instead of the thirty normal for public records.) Among the minor changes introduced to the form during this period was the question first asked in 1891 in Welsh counties concerning the ability of each person aged three or above to speak Welsh.

It is now possible in all counties to work on microfilm (or, for 1891, microfiche) copies of the enumerators' books in a local repository and avoid a visit to London; conversely, it is possible to look at the census for anywhere in England and Wales at the recently established Family Records Centre in central London, which has replaced the facilities at the now closed Chancery Lane branch of the PRO (pp. 150-1). The books are arranged according to the administrative geography of the Registrar General's department at the time of the census in question, in which the basic division of the country was into 'registration counties' (which do not correspond entirely with geographical counties) and then superintendent registrars' districts, registrars' sub-districts and finally enumeration districts. In country areas, the last was usually a parish or township, or a parish might contain two districts; in towns a block of streets would be allocated to a single enumerator. In either case, the area had to be small enough for one person to walk or ride round in a single evening, first distributing and then collecting the schedules.

Having collected the forms, and helped householders who were illiterate to fill them in, the enumerator copied each form into a book containing similarly ruled pages, drawing a line across the page at the end of each household. At the front of the book were pages on which the boundaries of the enumeration district were described and the number of people enumerated was tabulated. The enumerator had also to explain any special surplus or deficiency or population in his district that night, such as the presence of railway navvies or the temporary removal of a platoon of soldiers. It has always been the Registrar General's policy to enumerate the *de facto* population of a district, rather than who 'should' have been there. Finally, the enumerator signed his book as being as correct as he could make it and sent it to the local registrar, who checked all the books for his sub-district and sent them on to the superintendent. Eventually the books, now bearing three signatures as to accuracy, were forwarded to the Registrar General in London, where the numerical data (but not the names) was analysed and the results published in a series of massive volumes presented to Parliament as sessional papers (p. 156). These reports, which are available in the larger public libraries, contain basic statistics for the population of every township and parish in the country, with more sophisticated figures on occupation and birthplace published for the larger units, such as registration districts or counties. For the same information for smaller places, as well as details of individuals, one has to turn to the enumerators' books themselves.

The detail which can be extracted from the enumerators' books about a community of any size is almost endless, especially as six sets of books are now available, covering the period 1841-91. All the series are well preserved, although there are some gaps in the material for 1861 and occasional books missing for other years. For most purposes the 1841 census is less useful than the later ones because of the imprecise information collected about place of birth ('Were you born in this county, yes or no?', instead of 'Name the county and parish in which you were born') and imprecise age-reporting, where respondents had to give their age to the multiple of five next below their actual age (i.e. someone aged 69 would have reported their age as 65, as would someone aged 65, 66, 67 or 68). All the earlier books tend to give only approximate addresses for households, with no house numbers in towns and no house names in villages. Beginners should beware of mistaking the running household number in the left-hand column of the book (i.e. the number that goes from 1 to *n* throughout the book) for a house number, where the second column contains the name of a street. Thus '60 Wellington Street' only means No 60, Wellington Street if all that information appears in the second column; if it is divided between the first two then 60 is the number of the household and the address is merely somewhere in Wellington Street.

Apart from this trap, one of the attractions of the enumerators' books is the lack of technical problems. All the columns are clearly headed and the handwriting is usually fairly easy to read. Some occupations need a little effort to distinguish ('carrier' and 'currier', or 'chairwoman' and 'charwoman' for example) and phonetically spelt names of distant parishes of birth may require imagination as well as Bartholomew's *Gazetteer* to identify. This last column tends to be the least well completed, since many respondents believed that 'Ireland' was a county or that 'London' was a single parish. One also finds 'British Subject' in that column for people perhaps born to parents serving overseas during the Napoleonic Wars (1793-1815) who wished to make their nationality clear. 'N.K.' for 'Not Known' can occur for either the parish or county in the same column and occasionally in other columns. Otherwise, abbreviations such as 'Ag. Lab.' for agricultural labourer or 'D.S.' for domestic servant soon become obvious, while professional qualifications (usually medical) reduced to initials can be identified from a dictionary. Abbreviations for long disbanded service corps can be more of problem. Sometimes, despite the care with which the census seems generally to have been taken, one finds obvious mistakes, such as the transposition of information between columns or a patently impossible combination of age, sex, marital status or occupation, which has escaped the notice of the Registrar General's checkers.

Some investigators use census records merely to locate their own or another family, since the returns contain such invaluable genealogical information as age and birthplace, as well as providing a cross-section picture of a complete household; or to discover who was living in their house on census night in a particular year. Others may wish to use the books as part of a general study of a whole community, in which case they will probably do well to obtain a complete copy of the returns for their parish. Like the tithe map (p. 93), the census enumerators' books are so useful that it is worth sinking some money into the acquisition of full copies. While for a small village one can transcribe the schedules from one census in perhaps an afternoon (preferably using a home-made form similar to the original), for a larger place photocopies are probably the answer. Most libraries and record offices which have enumerators' books on microfilm also have reader-printers from which reasonably legible working copies can be made, although in some cases the film from which the prints are produced may be showing signs of age and heavy use. The Family Records Centre can also supply hard copy from census microfilm, although the cost will usually be greater.

Having made a complete copy of one or more enumerators' books for your chosen area, whether it is a village, suburb or just a particularly interesting street, you can proceed in one of two directions. The statistically minded may wish to produce figures for a small area comparable to those published for larger units in the census reports, such as the number of people born in different counties, a breakdown of the population by age and sex, or an occupational analysis of the community. This is a useful approach in identifying fairly precisely some of the leading features of a community (the exact importance of a particular trade in a one-industry town, or the number of Irish immigrants) but after a time diminishing returns set in. Average household size, for instance, while easy enough to calculate for anywhere from the enumerators' books, does not vary greatly between different parts of the country, nor do other aspects of nineteenth-century family structure. Your town or village is unlikely to differ very far from the norm, while for other variables (such as birthplace) the sample may be too small to be useful.

An alternative approach is to look at a community as individuals, rather than columns in a bar-graph or slices in a pie-chart. This one can do with a village or street or, with group effort, a small town. One can take all the members of a particular occupational group and see what common characteristics they had (were the farmers born locally?; were railway navvies mostly Irish?); one can look at the social composition of particular streets (a high incidence of lodgers and an absence of servants indicating relatively low status, with these two indicators reversed suggesting high status); or one can look at migration (e.g. a tenant farmer with several children all born in different parishes has obviously moved from farm to farm on annual tenancies and not been a long leaseholder at any). Almost all the information in an enumerator's book should suggest ideas to be explored in other ways (such as the prevailing type of farm tenancy, as in the last example), or to be examined over time by comparing one census with the next.

Another aspect of census analysis is to use the schedules in conjunction with a large-scale map of the district (most conveniently the tithe map for 1841 or 1851 and the second edition of the Ordnance Survey for 1861 and later), which makes it possible to give a geographical dimension to each of the questions posed of the material. With a contemporary map one can also try to locate on the ground each household in the census, a task dignified in academic circles as 'house repopulation' but which in most amateur projects is simply an entertaining (and sometimes frustrating) exercise in seeing who one's neighbours were a century ago. Some of the practical difficulties of this work are outlined in the chapter on maps (pp. 101-2).

Conclusion

With this introduction to the value of the census enumerators' books for nineteenth-century local history we have completed a brief tour of the material with which most investigators make a start. Some libraries will have more than what is described here, others will have less. In most parts of the country the resources of the nearest library can be supplemented by a major public library whose holdings are regional in scope. Occasionally a university library may augment public library holdings, but in general the latter are the specialists in this field. Most local studies libraries have leaflets on popular research topics or simply on how to use the library; their reference departments will have general books on subjects which you may wish to study in a local context; and the lending library should have the main local history, genealogical and archaeological textbooks.

As this chapter has tried to show, it is usually better to start research at the library rather than the record office: books are easier to read than most documents, library arrangements are more familiar to the beginner than the organisation of even a small record office, and you may as well see what other people have written about your parish before deciding what you are going to do yourself. On a more practical level, libraries tend to be open in the evenings and for at least part of Saturday, which is when most amateur researchers can get into them; archive services generally work a five-day week. Finally, work on printed sources in a library, plus some of the semi-archival material described here, provides a good grounding in how to make notes, how to chase up references and how to appreciate the way in which local historians draw on each other's work. Working in the opposite direction, one eventually gets back to a reference to a primary source which has to be followed up in a record office.

CHAPTER THREE

At the Record Office

Local archive services

Whereas many local studies libraries are over a century old, the same is not true of county or city record offices. Concern about the preservation even of official local records followed well behind that for the archives of central government which prompted the establishment of the Public Record Office in 1838. Only after 1918 did most county councils use powers they had possessed since 1889 to make provision for their own records and those of the court of quarter sessions which preceded them. About a dozen counties set up record offices before the Second World War, looking after the authority's own records, taking in material from defunct minor authorities, receiving some 'deposits' (i.e. long-term but revocable loans) of family and estate material or solicitors' papers, and possibly acting as the diocesan record office for the local bishop. After 1945 many more offices were established, until on the eve of local government reorganisation in 1974 the West Riding of Yorkshire had the unique distinction among English county councils (shared with some in rural Wales) of not providing an archive service.

Outside the metropolitan counties, the main consequence of the changes of 1974 was that large quantities of district council records were transferred from authorities which were then being abolished to county record offices. The counties themselves were not greatly affected and the new districts in general did not establish record offices, although some of those which inherited archive services from former county boroughs continued to maintain them. All but one of the short-lived metropolitan counties, set up in 1974 and wound up only twelve years later, did establish record offices, whereas the West Midlands continued to rely on Birmingham City Library and the smaller repositories in the region. The abolition of the metropolitan counties has left a situation in these areas (Merseyside, Greater Manchester, West Yorkshire, South Yorkshire and Tyne & Wear) comparable to that which has long existed in the West Midlands, with records scattered between a number of repositories in a distinctly unsatisfactory fashion.

The recent piecemeal reorganisation of local government in some English counties, involving the establishment of 'unitary authorities' with powers comparable to the old county boroughs, threatens further damage to local archive services, should any of these new councils be tempted to establish record offices of their own. If ideas of this sort are carried into effect, existing county archive services, many of them already poorly funded by their authorities, will suffer further. The abolition in 1996 of the Welsh county councils, all of which ran record offices, admittedly of varying quality, has arguably led to a deterioration in the service in a part of the country where (in some areas at least) there was little to boast about to start with. What is needed are fewer, better resourced local record offices, not a growth of small-scale ventures which are unlikely to provide a decent service to the public or a worthwhile career for their staff.

The work of local record offices has grown enormously since pioneers such as F.G. Emmison were creating a new profession between the two World Wars. It has not changed greatly in scope. A county record office exists partly to provide an efficient records management service for other departments of the county council, to select modern records of the authority for preservation, and to make them available to searchers. In practice all county offices are also recognised by the Lord Chancellor as repositories for certain classes of what are legally 'public records' but are not kept centrally. The most important material of this kind is the records of quarter sessions, the partly administrative, partly judicial, body which until 1889 formed the top tier of local government in England and Wales and survived as a court until 1971. As well as looking after these, archive services have taken into custody records of other local authorities in their area, especially those which were abolished either in 1974 or at an earlier date.

The second major category of local record office holdings are the records of the Church of England from diocesan (or in York provincial) level downwards. All diocesan bishops in England have designated a local authority or university repository as their record office, to which have been transferred the administrative and judicial records of the bishop and such bodies as the dean and chapter from the middle ages almost to the present. Since 1979 it has been the policy of the church to encourage parishes to deposit their older registers and other ecclesiastical records in county offices, most of which are now in archival custody. In Wales the non-parochial records of the church are deposited at the National Library at Aberystwyth, while parish records may also go there or, as is more commonly the case in most of the province, to local offices. County record offices also have responsibility for inspecting and taking on deposit the records of the civil parishes set up in 1894 and the 'civil records of ecclesiastical parishes', which in many places were not separated from the church records in 1894 as they were supposed to be.

Thirdly, record offices receive on deposit, are given, or from time to time buy a variety of other material. In particular they have received from the landowning families of the county accumulations of manorial records, estate papers, political and personal papers and much else. Such deposits often contain hundreds, if not thousands, of deeds, as do those from solicitors which form probably the second largest class of deposited documents in most offices. Record offices also take in material from Nonconformist congregations, trade unions, businesses, voluntary organisations and individuals. This material is so heterogeneous as to be impossible to describe briefly, but it would be true to say that the records of landownership bulk largest among 'gifts, deposits and purchases'.

This outline of the contents of a typical county record office, like that of a local studies library, cannot explain in detail the considerable differences that exist between different counties. Some archive services run two or three branch offices, some do not have diocesan records, and all provide different levels of service to the public. In addition, some universities and many local studies libraries and museums, especially in large cities, also have archive collections, mainly because they were in existence long before county record offices. Thus in the West Riding, which had no archive service, Sheffield City Library became the natural repository for several major estate and business collections, some of them of national importance, from the south of the county. In this case, the library established an archives department as well as a local history department, which has in recent years been floated off as a separate organisation. In smaller libraries the local studies section, or just an interested librarian, took in documents that would otherwise have been destroyed. An alternative course which was followed in some cities, for example Bristol, Southampton and Hull, was for the county borough to set up a record office within the town clerk's department, initially to house its own records but also to take material on deposit.

Local government reorganisation in 1974 did not altogether accommodate the variations that had developed in archive services, even in the non-metropolitan counties, and over the last twenty years the picture has remained confused in some areas. Where a county library service absorbed one or more borough libraries in 1974, each with a small manuscript collection, these were sometimes quietly removed to the county record office. Partly because of local sensibilities, larger collections in former county borough libraries were less likely to be transferred, although the opportunity may have been taken to list documents properly for the first time, and in some old borough libraries record office staff identified important items among uncatalogued material. Both before 1974 and since there has been a tendency among archivists to criticise the way in which librarians look after archives; this should not, however, obscure the fact that had libraries not accepted the collections in the first place, perhaps during a war-time salvage drive, or gone out to country houses after the war and rescued tons of deeds and other papers, the documents would not now be there to squabble over. On the other hand, it cannot be emphasised too strongly that the re-emergence in some towns of a separate borough library service should not be used as an excuse to set up a record office as well.

A development since 1974 in a few counties has been the establishment of branch record offices in former borough libraries some distance from the county town, an acceptable arrangement as long as such enterprises remain branches of a unified county service. A more widespread practice has been the distribution of copies of parish registers, large-scale maps and other basic sources, either on microfilm or as full-size photocopies, to the principal branch libraries in the county, where they can be used alongside printed local studies material. Both policies are intended to relieve pressure that has built up on record office search-rooms since the late 1970s, especially from the large number of visitors interested in family history.

Making a start

A first visit to a record office is best prefaced not merely by reading something about record offices in general and studying a published guide or the introductory leaflet now issued by virtually all offices, but also by making an appointment and working out fairly clearly what you want to see. It is depressing for archivists to deal with searchers who have only come to look at printed books on the search-room shelves which they could see in their local library, or with people who haven't a clue what they will find in a record office. No-one expects beginners to know exactly what they are looking for, or to have a thorough knowledge of the office's holdings; the trick is to ask intelligent questions and to be able to ask for a couple of relevant things to start with. For this, an initial exchange of letters or a telephone call is best; in some offices it is virtually insisted upon because of pressure on seating or the need to bring documents from an outside store.

If you are interested in a rural parish, ask for brief details of the main collections in the office which relate to the place. For larger communities this approach will be unrealistic because the office will have dozens of references and it is better to explain what aspect of the town's history you are studying. For a particular industry, it is reasonable to ask what there is in the office, although in some cases this is either too general an enquiry (local offices in coalfields have tons of records from the National Coal Board, not always fully listed) or too specific (as in the case of an enquiry about viticulture in Victorian Glamorgan, which even the best arranged subject index would have difficulty answering). If you simply wish to confirm that a particular set of parish registers is in the office, or a tithe map, a phone call is enough to check that a seat will be available when you arrive, as well as the document. It is unfair to ask archivists to answer detailed enquiries over the phone, especially if they are on duty in the search-room at the same time. Equally, there is a limit, which appears to have narrowed in recent years, to the amount of help which archivists can give in replies to postal enquiries, for which some offices now make a charge based on the time taken to answer a letter.

Most archive services work a standard five-day week, although a few open one evening a week or one Saturday morning a month. Conversely, some offices only open to the public four days a week, an arrangement guaranteed to maximise irritation on the part of searchers in return for questionable savings to the local authority. For many local historians it is a lengthy journey just to get to the office, so make the most of your time. Arrive by appointment, preferably having ordered a few documents to start with (most offices will only produce a limited number at once). Do not come in even a small group without prior authority. Check beforehand if the record office can accommodate laptop computers;

unfortunately a few also allow the use of pocket dictating machines, which disturb other users (as do mobile phones, which should be banned from search-rooms). It is simplest just to bring one note-pad and several pencils, but not your own pencil sharpener, since the droppings fall on to documents and upset archivists, who also wince at the sight of readers rubbing out mistakes in their notes for the same reason.

An increasing number of local offices require the production (or issue) of a reader's ticket on arrival, as the Public Record Office has always done. Many accept a common 'CARN' (County Archive Research Network) document, which any participating office can issue on production of a driving licence or other identification. All offices ask readers to sign a visitor's book. Once you have signed in, found a seat and your documents, establish what local custom is for ordering more material. Some offices only bring documents from the strong-room at set intervals; if this is the case try to pace your work and have a supply of request slips ready to feed into the system, which will avoid the frustration of sitting there with nothing to look at while all around you are working away. If you do find yourself having to wait for material to be produced, it is always worth scanning the printed books on the search-room shelves or browsing through the finding-aids.

All record offices have certain common rules, with which beginners should be familiar before their first visit. Apart from such obvious courtesies as not eating in the search-room or talking more than necessary, the most fundamental regulations concern the welfare of the documents. All material that is produced in the search-room must be handled with the greatest care. Bound volumes should always be placed on stands or cushions rather than flat on a table; pages must be turned carefully. Under no circumstances should anything, especially sweaty hands but also notebooks, magnifying glasses or other impedimenta, be placed on the documents, which must not be piled on top of one another. If you are consulting a rolled map or other document that will not lie flat of its own accord, the staff will supply weights. If a bundle of deeds or other documents is produced in one go (which in practice tends not to be the case), make sure that the items stay in the same order as that in which they started and never unwrap a new bundle before securing the previous one. Above all, only pencil may be used to make notes and no mark of any kind may be made on a document.

Note-making and using the finding-aids

Apart from the fact that everything must be written in pencil, note-taking in record offices should be done in basically the same way as in libraries (p. 23). Head the page with the name of the office and the date of your visit, then write the reference number of the first document brought to you. The number will appear in a list or index and will also be written on the document itself. Unless you are editing the document for publication there is generally no need to make a literal transcript of the text—merely note points of interest. If the document is a volume in which the leaves are paginated or folioed these numbers should be noted in the same way as the pages of a printed book, although for records arranged chronologically, such as a parish register or a minute book, the date of an entry is usually a sufficient reference. As in a library, it is often a good idea of make a separate list of references from the finding-aids and to tick them off as you look at them.

If you arrive at the office having written first to ask what is available for a particular topic you will already have some leads, or you may be following up footnotes in VCH or other printed sources. Once you have looked at any documents suggested by the archivist you will probably be shown the office's finding-aids, from which your initial enquiry will have been answered. The arrangement of documents in record offices does not vary fundamentally from county to county, but the extent to which holdings have been catalogued does, largely as a function of what staff are available and how long the office has been in existence.

The basic threefold division of the holdings of most county record offices has already been described. This is normally reflected in the arrangement of the lists on the search-room shelves. The records of quarter sessions will most commonly be described first, then the diocesan records, then the deposited or transferred material. Some offices divide the last category by subject, so that there will be a series of lists of district council records, another of family and estate collections, one of business records and so on. Perhaps a more common system, although it may seem less helpful to the user, is for all the deposits to be numbered from 1 onwards (usually prefaced by D for Deposit), or to be given a mnemonic reference and the lists arranged alphabetically by this reference. Thus in Lincolnshire the muniments of Lord Ancaster have references beginning ANC, while in Nottingham-shire those of the Dukes of Portland are DDP; by contrast Derbyshire and Staffordshire both use a running serial number system.

The official records will be arranged according to 'administrative provenance'. Thus quarter sessions records are normally divided into those created by each of the chief officers of the county (clerk of the peace, county treasurer, county surveyor etc.). The model arrangement of diocesan records followed by most offices is similar, if rather more complex because of the mixture of judicial and administrative functions exercised by a bishop. With the deposited records, gifts and purchases the fundamental principle is to keep each collection separate because of its separate provenance. Even if it consists of only one item it is not bulked together with other small accessions. Some deposits have a clear internal arrangement, as with local authority records. Alternatively, the documents may have arrived not merely unsorted but disarranged, as in the case of a country house collection which has spent many years in a leaking conservatory, or a solicitor's collection where different clients' papers have been mixed together. Here, apart from physically conserving the material, the archivist's task is to try to discern an order beneath the superficial chaos and catalogue the collection in that order. In an estate collection, deeds will be separated from rentals and surveys and usually arranged by place; official correspondence about the lord lieutenancy will be listed separately from private letters.

Once a collection has been sorted the next step is to list it, although most offices have a backlog of unlisted collections. Completed lists are put on the search-room shelves (except in the case of modern or confidential records not immediately available to the public) and it is these the searcher consults. Search-room lists vary a good deal in the amount of detail they provide as to the contents of the collection, but as a minimum will give the searcher a reference number by which to order a particular item and probably some idea of its contents. A 'piece' thus ordered may be a volume, a sheet of paper or a parchment roll. On the other hand, a list is not the same as a 'calendar', a detailed summary of the contents of a document. In the case of most deposited material, a list should provide sufficient information for the searcher to establish whether it is likely to be useful. Thus a list of business records (say ledgers or letter-books) will give the covering dates of each volume. Rentals in an estate collection will be listed so that one can see which parishes or manors are covered.

In one particular case a search-room list may be sufficiently detailed to make it unnecessary to send for the original. This is where a collection of deeds has been listed (or, to be precise, calendared) so as to include all the material information. Most offices try to catalogue medieval deeds in this way, because few searchers can read the originals (which are in Latin in a difficult hand). For later deeds, some collections may have been treated in the same detail, but few offices can list eighteenth- and nineteenth-century deeds so fully. They may merely note the parties to each deed and the places mentioned, or only prepare a list which identifies the contents of each box ('Bedfordshire, 1650-1900; Bucks., 13th cent.-1550', and so on). Here the searcher has no choice but to get the box out and go through it piece by piece.

Some local historians using county record offices are interested in particular subjects across all or part of the county; for them a folder of lists bringing together all the urban district council records may be exactly what they want for their study of late nineteenth-century local government. If, however, they are working in an office which does not arrange its lists by subject, such searchers will have to rely on a subject index, usually on cards (a few offices now have computer-printed or on-line databases), to identify relevant collections. However the deposited records are arranged, searchers interested in a particular parish, family or individual will turn first not to the lists, unless they have been given some leads by the staff, but to the personal and place-name indexes. In an ideal office, all the names and places which appear in the lists will have been indexed, and all the collections will have been listed. In most offices, by no means all the collections have been listed, and by no means all the lists have been indexed. But as a start, look at the index under the place or person in which you are interested and follow the references there back to the relevant list. If the description in the list suggests the document will be useful, send for it. On the other hand, archivists generally do not care for searchers who simply copy references from the indexes straight on to request slips; check the context first.

Understanding local records

Much of this chapter has so far been devoted to how a record office organises its holdings, because this is precisely what a new visitor to a search-room often fails to understand. Record offices do not house a mass of undifferentiated documents out of which archivists somehow produce what you are looking for, or tell you they have nothing relevant; their holdings have come into the office from a variety of sources, some have been examined in more detail than others, and some parts of the county will be better documented than others. The lists and indexes are a partial but not complete guide. For example, just because a particular person does not appear in the name index this does not mean that there is nothing about him in the office. If he was a criminal he may feature in quarter sessions records; if he was a pauper there may be an unindexed removal order in a parish collection; if he had business dealings with a firm whose records are in the office he may appear in their ledgers. The same is true of any parish in the county. It is certainly the case that some parishes have better family and estate collections than others, and not all parish registers are equally well preserved. But all parishes feature in quarter sessions records and there will be something about most country parishes in the records of the relevant rural district council. To make full use of a county record office one must appreciate how its contents have been catalogued and, above all, the background history of the place, person or subject you are interested in, as well as the history of local administration which has created the records.

It would be impossible, even if the whole of this book was devoted to the holdings of a local record office, to go into great detail about the sources to be found there for every possible topic which a local historian might wish to pursue. What is perhaps best, in a book aimed at beginners, is to concentrate on a limited number of basic sources which present comparatively few technical problems and from which one can discover a good deal fairly quickly about almost anywhere, urban or rural. The focus in this section is mainly the parish, which remains the most meaningful unit in country areas to the present day for local administration and life generally (in Wales as well as England, even though civil parishes in Wales are now called 'communities'). The parish has considerably less relevance in towns or in rural communities which have become suburbs, but until the nineteenth century it was still the only unit of local government below county level and the one through which quarter sessions and central government executed policy or collected information. Library and record office catalogues are usually arranged by parish, as are many printed sources. At an early stage in any project, whether it is the general history of a community or something more specific, it is important to establish the parochial geography of the area you are interested in.

One important qualification to this emphasis is necessary in the North of England and most of Wales, where the civil functions of ecclesiastical parishes (chiefly the relief of the poor and maintenance of highways) were discharged by subdivisions of parishes called 'townships' or 'hamlets'. Generally it was they, and not the vast, thinly populated parishes, which were the fundamental units of local organisation and which for this reason were adopted in 1894 as the basis of the system of civil parishes throughout England and Wales.

Another important point is that it is unwise to think in terms, rather as J.C. Cox's manual did, of writing a continuous history of your parish from 1086 to the present. For most parishes there is very little material in record offices before 1550; what there is is probably written in Latin and beyond the expertise of most amateurs. Usually, most of what can be discovered of their medieval history derives from central government archives. For the 'early modern' period, between about 1550 and 1750, there is a wealth of material in English local record offices (much less in Wales), but although most records were by then kept in English they are still written in a hand that needs some practice to master, especially before 1660. It may be fun to learn 'secretary hand' in an evening class from clear examples explained by a good tutor; it is dispiriting for beginners to be given a document in a record office of which they are unable to read a single word, or to spend pounds on photocopies of sixteenth-century material which after hours of study still remains largely baffling. It is much better to start with straightforward post-1750 documents and to work backwards rather than forwards. Archive material from this period also ties in more readily with what you are likely to have gleaned from printed sources.

Local administration: parish and township

A good starting point may well be local government records. Leaving aside for a moment the medieval chartered boroughs, some of which survived into modern times as local authorities which may have inherited richer source material for their earlier history, local government before the mid nineteenth century was undertaken by two main agencies: the county, through quarter sessions, and the parish (or township). While it is worth checking any indexes to quarter sessions material that are available, it is probably best to start with the parish and then look at the new statutory undertakings which replaced it during the nineteenth century.

Since early medieval times England has been divided into parishes, which form the lowest tier in a hierarchy of ecclesiastical administration that leads through the rural deanery to the archdeaconry, the diocese and thence the provinces of Canterbury and York. Its best known records are the registers ordered to be kept in 1538 of all baptisms, burials and marriages in the parish, which have long formed the staple diet of genealogists and more recently have been extensively used for work on local population history. Only in a comparatively small number of parishes do registers survive from 1538, although for many English parishes they start before 1600. In Wales, the starting date may be as late as 1750. Their use for both genealogy and population history has been explained many times elsewhere; their value for more general community studies may be more limited, unless the earlier volumes contain a good deal of annotation as well as simply recording vital events.

In the sixteenth century the parish (or township) was adopted by parliament as the unit within which two basic aspects of local adminis-tration were to be discharged: the relief of the poor and the upkeep of the highways. In each community unpaid officials were appointed annually as overseers of the poor and surveyors of highways, in addition to the two churchwardens who were responsible, with the incumbent, for the maintenance of the church itself. A constable was also appointed with nominal responsibility for law and order and a rather more substantial obligation for central government tax collection, in a hierarchy of civil officers which passed through the high constable of each hundred (or wapentake) and the sheriff of the county to the Exchequer in London, where the records of this aspect of his work have ended up.

Each of these sets of officers (overseers, surveyor, churchwardens and constable) had power to levy a rate to support their work, and all were supposed to keep accounts of its collection and disbursement. For the overseers this meant paying out doles to the poor, meeting the expense of removing as many paupers as possible to another parish, and perhaps in the eighteenth century contributing to the maintenance of a local workhouse. The surveyor's accounts either list payments to contractors for the repair of roads, paid out of the rates, or record work done by ratepayers themselves to save the expense of paying outside labour. The churchwardens disbursed their rates not merely on routine items such as washing cassocks or removing polecats from the steeple, but from time to time had to pay for major repairs to the church or even partial rebuilding, in which case the accounts may supply the name of an architect. Constables' accounts usually record only the routine expenses of office.

Accounts such as these may survive from the sixteenth or seventeenth century in well documented parishes; even in less fortunate places there should be some material for the last few decades of the old system. The poor law was reformed in 1834, highways administration a year later, while compulsory church rates, which the wardens collected and disbursed, ended in 1868. While the outgoings in any surviving account books illustrate how the parish was administered by its unpaid and often reluctant officers, the lists of ratepayers (by the nineteenth century kept in separate ratebooks) may be useful in identifying who was living in the larger houses which tend to be named separately in the lists. Quite commonly, prior to about 1820, all the parish accounts were kept in a single book (the 'township book' in some northern communities) and the same small group of men discharged all the offices year after year.

The various officials were responsible to a general meeting of parishioners, known from its nominal meeting place as 'the vestry', although meetings were often adjourned to a pub. Anyone, whether or not they were churchgoers, could attend the vestry until its reorganisation in 1920, but usually only a handful of families were represented. In the early nineteenth century, especially in industrialising parishes, ratepayers realised that some sort of executive was needed to make parochial legislation work and a 'select vestry' evolved, acting as a *de facto* local council for what may by this date have been quite a large town. Such bodies, which varied from the highly efficient to the hopelessly corrupt, usually kept minutes, as did some ordinary vestries by the eighteenth century, and through these one can trace the efforts of the ratepayers to organise local administration. From the 1830s, however, new bodies gradually removed all effective power from the parishes.

Before outlining the material likely to be available for later nineteenth-century local government, it may be worth saying something about the other strictly ecclesiastical records of parishes besides registers. As they lost their general administrative functions to elected boards, Anglican parishes became far more energetic in their cure of souls, and this is often reflected in their records. The middle decades of the century saw a great deal of church restoration, the building of mission churches, the division of over-large parishes into new districts, and the founding of church schools. This may have left a legacy of minute books (of building committees, restoration committees or school managers), accounts, or printed ephemera recording the laying of foundation stones or the opening of new buildings. It may be of interest to see, using directories in conjunction with parish records, what sort of people were supporting the church in this work; where Nonconformist records also survive from the same community one can compare the progress of church and chapel and identify who supported which party.

Poor relief

The first major reform of local government concerned the poor law, which, especially in southern England, became the target of much well merited criticism in the early nineteenth century. In an effort to reduce rates and make the system more efficient, responsibility (except for actually collecting rates) was removed from parishes to elected 'boards of guardians of the poor' serving a 'union' of parishes. This body was made responsible for building and running a union workhouse, usually in a conveniently located town at the centre of the district, to which surrounding rural parishes were to send their poor. Outdoor relief was in fact never entirely ended and the system was greatly modified before its final abolition in 1930, when the guardians' powers (and thus their records) passed to county and county borough councils, while many workhouses became hospitals.

County record offices should have, for most if not all the unions in their area, minutes and possibly other records from shortly after 1834 to 1930. From the minutes one can see the earliest of the new local government bodies working to enforce the Poor Law Amendment Act in their union, building a workhouse, appointing a master and matron, establishing policy and adapting to later legislative changes. For the workhouse itself there may be such human documents as diet sheets or admission and discharge books listing inmates who passed through the institution. While the interest of this material for the historian of a rural parish on the edge of the union may be limited, for anyone working on a town in which a workhouse was situated guardians' minutes are of value not merely for their administrative content but also because they recapture the political life of the time. Election contests can be followed in local newspapers as well as the minutes of the board.

Education

The pattern set by the Poor Law Amendment Act, of a small central government department overseeing the work of elected local boards charged with a single task, was followed later in the nineteenth century by reforms in other areas of social policy. One such field, which again creates a large body of readily accessible material for the local historian, is education. Although the government, through a committee of the Privy Council, had been disbursing grants from the 1830s to voluntary bodies (Anglican and Nonconformist) working to make elementary education more widely available, it was not until 1870 that an Act provided for the creation of elected school boards in places where voluntary provision was inadequate. Elementary education was later made first compulsory and then free, and by the end of the century it was clear that rate-supported schools would become the main providers, replacing voluntary bodies. It also became clear that the local school boards, whose view of their functions often remained depressingly narrow, should be replaced by larger bodies. Thus in 1902 the education committees of county and county borough councils, and of the larger municipal boroughs and urban district councils, took the place of the boards. The minor authorities survived the reform of 1944 but in 1974 education outside London was placed entirely in the hands of county council and metropolitan districts, so that most surviving records should now have reached county record offices.

School board records, like most local government material, consist of minutes, sometime interspersed with annual reports of the clerk to the board (the predecessor of the post-1902 education officer), from which one can study the struggle to provide a universal system of elementary education between the 1870s and the turn of the century. The proposed creation of a board under the 1870 Act often triggered a great deal of local strife, as ratepayers fought to keep out yet another rate-supported body, Churchmen fought against 'secular' elementary education, and Nonconformists wanted to establish schools run by other than Anglicans. As with guardians' elections, it is worth pursuing school board politics through the local press, especially at times when it is obvious from the minutes that there was bitter conflict on the board. Occasionally, when the records of a church school have survived, it may be possible to look at both sides of a dispute, as the Church party fought first to prevent the creation of a school board, then to secure a majority on the board, and last of all to obstruct its attempts to take over their schools.

Material may also have reached the county record office from the schools themselves, usually in the form of log books kept by head-teachers and returned to the authority when the school shut. Detailed log books can provide a colourful picture of late nineteenth-century school life and have been the mainstay of many centenary histories, although in some counties they are closed for longer than the usual 30 years because of the personal nature of the contents. In some counties, schools that are still open retain their older log books, while in others they are transferred to archival custody.

Public health and the district councils

Poor law and education were two fields in which specially elected bodies were established by Parliament; while they were evolving there was a parallel process, concerned initially with public health reform, which gradually broadened into the kind of modern local government below county level that was swept away in 1974.

The first effective Public Health Act dates from 1848. It was adoptive, that is, ratepayers could choose whether or not to establish a local board of health. Most did not, except in the new industrial towns where the vestry was now ineffective as a local authority. Here, and in some older towns where a chartered borough became the local board, the Act was adopted and a board elected, whose minutes may survive from soon after 1848. So also should a report on the health of the district prepared as part of the setting-up process, which often provides a comprehensive and lurid account of ill-health, poor housing, insanitary drainage and administrative inaction. These reports were printed and may be found in local libraries as well as record offices; the Department of Health (as the successor central department) also has a set.

Neither the initiative of 1848, nor a later Act of 1858, was universally adopted and it was not until 1871-5 that three comprehensive statutes established local sanitary authorities throughout the country, responsible to a much stronger central body, the Local Government Board. In rural areas the poor law guardians were at first responsible for public health under this reform, but in small towns, mining or industrial villages, or new suburbs where more action was needed, new 'local boards' were elected. Despite their title, they were at first concerned mainly with public health and only in 1894, when they were remodelled as urban district councils (and at the same time the guardians' public health responsibilities were transferred to separately elected rural district councils), did they take on wider responsibilities. The largest became elementary education authorities in 1902; most built houses to rent after 1919 (and in some cases from an earlier date).

UDC and RDC records were some of the bulkiest new accessions received by county record offices during the reorganisation of 1972-4, even allowing for the amount that was destroyed either by retiring members and officers bitter at their councils' abolition or by archivists overwhelmed by furniture vans full of ratebooks. Since 1974 they have probably been among the least used modern records in local offices and have been seen as distinctly unglamorous. The old district councils were not for the most part very exciting institutions; few spent their ratepayers' money with the abandon of their successors and their records may seem of little interest. But it is worth checking from a directory when the local board in a small town or mining village was established and looking at its minutes. Once again, one can identify the personalities behind early local government and retrace the struggle to clean up industrial communities in the late nineteenth century. From the end of the First World War their records become an important source for the history of council housing.

County councils, parish councils and boroughs

The minutes and reports of the county councils established by the Local Government Act of 1888 (except early 'verbatim reports') are often too general to be of interest to historians of particular communities, although where files relating to particular services survive (e.g. education) they may be worth consulting. The county councils celebrated their first half century in 1939 by producing a set of uniform handbooks, half of each book containing a standard account of county government since 1889 cast in the 'Fifty Glorious Years' mould, and the second half consisting of short accounts of each major committee of the authority whose name and arms were stamped on the front cover. They are interesting period pieces, and a useful guide to the pre-war functions and outlook of the county councils. Some, but by no means all, the counties produced rather more lavish centenary histories in 1989; a few of those that fell from grace in 1974, notably the West Riding, were the subject of 'In Memoriam' volumes around that time.

The powers given to the parish councils and parish meetings set up in 1894 were so limited that their records are often dismissed as lacking any historical interest. This may be true, although they were essentially the successors of the earlier vestry meetings and their minutes help to convey an impression of village life, and the preoccupations of its more active citizens, over the last century.

Those towns which trace their administrative history from a medieval borough charter stand a little apart from the local authorities so far described, although their modern records are largely similar. Despite their mayor and aldermen, separate commission of the peace, charters and coats of arms, all of which counted for naught in 1974, most trace their modern history from the adoption of the 1848 Public Health Act or one of the later reforms. The Municipal Corporations Act of 1835 merely provided for a proper system of election of members, appointment of officers and audit of accounts. Except for police powers, it did not lay any new duties on boroughs. Before 1835 surviving borough records may include minutes of some kind of 'town council' (which may go under any of several names), accounts, and deeds and other papers concerned with borough property. Few boroughs enjoyed much administrative vitality in the eighteenth century, even those with their own court of quarter sessions, and their records tend to be correspondingly dull. For the larger towns of pre-industrial England, and a few of the smaller boroughs, there may be very rich early modern material in a local record office, as well as medieval charters establishing the burgesses' privileges in the first place. This material has usually been well catalogued and is often partly accessible in print through record publications.

The 1888 Local Government Act, as well as setting up county councils, also created the county boroughs in their modern form, large towns whose corporations enjoyed all the powers of both county councils and urban sanitary authorities and were responsible for all local government services in their area. These authorities were abolished in 1974, although the winding-up of the metropolitan counties in 1986 left the metropolitan districts as county boroughs in all but name. The same is also true of the unitary authorities which replaced county and district councils in Wales in 1996 and in parts of England in 1997-8. County borough council records are similar in character to those of non-county boroughs, although larger in bulk and probably generally better preserved. They also include material from borough education committees from 1902 (dealing with technical and secondary as well as elementary education) and public assistance committees from 1930, which have no parallel among the archives of the non-county boroughs or urban districts. In non-metropolitan counties, former county borough records should now be in county record offices, except where there is a city record office run by the successor district; in practice they have tended to stay put since 1974 to a greater extent than is the case with the records of the smaller authorities.

The archives of the statutory local authorities, especially for a small town or a suburb, provide a good picture of how nineteenth-century administration worked and enlarge a picture of the community obtained from printed sources. Before going any further back, local historians seeking material on an urban community, and to a lesser extent a rural parish, may wish to see whether the record office has received deposits from other nineteenth-century institutions, such as Nonconformist congregations, trade union branches or friendly societies. This material, which is roughly similar in character to that created by local authorities but far less bulky and less well preserved, will further amplify what has been discovered from local authority records of the last century or so of life in a community, without requiring any special expertise in reading the documents or understanding their contents.

Landownership and the history of houses

Having exhausted the scope of administrative records, the local historian may well turn next to the mass of material generated by landownership, whether of rural or urban property, which bulks very large in the holdings of all county record offices. Here the essential starting-point is to find out who owned the land in the parish in which you are interested at some date in the past. This can be done quickly from a directory (p. 29) or more thoroughly from the tithe map of the 1840s (p. 93) or an earlier inclosure award (p. 102). It is now possible also to obtain details of current ownership from the Land Registry for property to which the title has been registered, whereas historically the Registry was closed to public search. Present-day ownership may help with an historical enquiry but for most purposes it is probably best to start with a mid nineteenth-century source (ideally the tithe map), since there may be no easy way of going back from the present day through several rapid changes of ownership in recent years to a date at which archive material becomes available.

There will be many instances where it is difficult to make progress even with details from the tithe map. The pattern of landownership in the nineteenth century varied greatly between different parts of England and Wales and within a single county. The most convenient case is one where a single family enjoyed a long period of ownership of most or all of a parish, preferably including the lordship of a manor, and that family has since disposed of its property and handed over estate papers to the record office. This is by no means a common state of affairs. Even if landownership was dominated by a single family its records may have been largely or wholly destroyed. Even if it has well preserved muniments they may still be at the estate office, where local historians may or may not be welcome. Alternatively, the parish may have been a peripheral part of an estate centred in another part of the country, with the muniments of the entire estate deposited in a distant county record office. Another possibility is that the Crown, through the Duchy of Lancaster or the Duchy of Cornwall, for example, has been the major historic owner (p. 145). The nineteenth-century owner may have been a recent purchaser of an estate and have inherited or kept nothing belonging to his predecessor. The parish may have been fairly evenly divided between several middling estates, none of which have much in the way of surviving muniments, or the parish may have lacked any dominant landowner but had numerous resident freeholders. These are all points worth bearing in mind before berating the staff of the record office for failing to have any family or estate material for your parish.

Personal enquiry and a search of the indexes should locate any material at the local record office; often the staff will know from previous enquiries whether there are any collections elsewhere or, if muniments are still in private hands, will advise on how, if at all, the owner should be approached for access. A more systematic way of obtaining the same two pieces of information is to write to the National Register of Archives (Quality Court, Chancery Lane, London WC2A 1HP). This is a small official body which does not collect documents itself but builds up lists of collections, either through the work of its own staff or in collaboration with record repositories, and can help in tracking down fugitive archives. If you are specifically interested in locating manorial records (with which in practice are often to be found other records of landownership) ask for details (of particular parishes, rather than larger areas) from the NRA's Manorial Documents Register. For anyone with the chance to visit London, all this can be done in person at Quality Court during office hours.

Assuming there is an estate collection in the record office for your parish, what is it likely to contain? A good collection should include deeds recording the purchase or disposal of all or part of the estate; leases to tenants of land, farms and houses within it; rentals and surveys listing tenants, their holdings and the terms on which the premises were held; and, if you are lucky, estate maps. These are discussed more fully in Chapter 4 (p. 107) but are generally on a large scale, marking individual fields, which are numbered and keyed to a written schedule ('terrier'), to be found either alongside or in a separate book. From this you can get an overall view of the estate at a particular date, and if you are very lucky there may be two or three surveys a generation or more apart, enabling you to compare the growth or decline of the estate, or the appearance or disappearance of buildings, even of whole villages. If the map has been lost but the terrier remains, it should still be possible to look at change on the estate by comparing farm sizes and tenants' names. If one of the surveys dates from the 1840s or later it should be possible to compare it with both the tithe map and the census enumerators' books (pp. 93, 35) to build up a picture of the estate in the nineteenth century. Where an entire estate was offered for sale at a particular date, for example just after the First World War, there should be a printed sale catalogue (possibly in the local studies library rather than the record office) which is likely to be so detailed as to provide another complete survey of the estate, this time at the end its life.

To analyse a series of estate surveys thoroughly, or to compare them with other sources, really involves transcribing the entire survey and copying any maps. The names of the tenants and their holdings can then be matched against other references, this being another instance, as with information from directories, where a slip index or computer database may be useful. Analysis of this sort should make it possible to study a whole parish, or a large part of a parish, in some detail, especially between the eighteenth century and the early twentieth. The same sources can be used on a smaller scale by those interested in tracing the history of their own (or anyone else's) house.

Depending on the detail with which rentals and surveys have been compiled, it may be possible to link deeds from elsewhere in the collection with holdings listed in other records. The leases or other agreements by which tenants held their property may survive (and can be linked to rentals by checking names of parties and farms); some surveys may identify from whom the estate acquired the property while the deeds recording the purchase may also be preserved.

All record offices have large quantities of deeds, mainly acquired from solicitors, which are not part of an estate collection but may include property in the parish in which you are interested. Make a note of the basic details of the deed and see if at some stage you can identify the property on a large-scale plan or in a rental or survey. As already suggested (pp. 48-9), it is often possible to rely merely on a record office list for the salient points of a deed, much of which is common form. There are reliable manuals on the use of deeds by local historians (see Further Reading) but three of the most common types of post-medieval conveyance should perhaps be explained here.

A freehold conveyance, i.e. outright sale from A to B, was most often effected from the sixteenth to the nineteenth centuries by one of two procedures: bargain and sale or (in the second half of the period) lease and release. In both, the deed opens with the date and the names of the parties, in simple cases the name of the vendor followed by that of the purchaser. Then comes the 'consideration' (the price paid for the property), followed by the clause which defines the type of conveyance (bargain and sale or lease and release), followed by a description of the property, introduced by the phrase 'All that ... '. When you come to the next standard formula, 'To have and to hold ... ', you can very often stop, since, mortgages and settlements apart, the rest is common form. The two types of freehold conveyance differed in phrase but not in intent. A bargain and sale was the more straightforward and was what its name implied; a lease and release was slightly more devious, consisting of a lease (i.e. the disposal of the property for a temporary period, in this case normally a year), followed a day later by a 'release' in which (in simple terms) the lessor of the previous day's deed gave up his right to recover the property from the lessee, making the conveyance equivalent to a bargain and sale. The two deeds were generally folded inside one another; problems occasionally arise in spotting that a lease is in fact preliminary to a release when the latter has been lost.

The third type of document found very commonly in solicitors' or estate collections is a lease in the normal sense, in which an owner let property either for a year or a term of years (commonly seven or a multiple thereof) or for a term of lives (usually three). Here the lease opens in the same way a freehold conveyance, with the date, names of the parties and description of the property, the latter preceded by the formula 'Hath sett to farm' or 'Hath to farm let', which confirms that the document is a lease. Then will come the period for which the lease is to run and the annual rent, followed by 'reservations' to the landlord (most often of woods and minerals on or under the property) and then other special conditions ('covenants'). One particular type of lease, found chiefly in certain large towns in the nineteenth century, usually has a large number of detailed covenants. This is the ninety-nine-year building lease, by which estates sold plots to developers, who were required to erect houses on the land according to precise provisions concerning their size and shape; the builder could then sell the houses but at the end of ninety-nine years both the plot and the buildings standing on it reverted to the ground landlord, who had in the meantime collected a nominal ground (or quit) rent from the property. Where the term of a lease is very long (999 years, or even 2,000, as occurs occasionally) the conveyance amounts to a sale of the freehold, even though the deed is cast is in the form of a lease. In this case, later transfers of the property are by means of an assignment of the lease from the vendor to the purchaser for the period of years remaining unexpired out of the original term.

There are numerous other types of title deed, and the documents tend to become physically larger and more complex down to the end of the nineteenth century, and thus more offputting. If they have not been listed in detail by the record office, either ignore them, or sit in front of them with one of the textbooks until the important features begin to stand out from the common form. As already explained, medieval deeds written in Latin are usually calendared in full and may well have been published by record societies or munificent nineteenth-century owners.

Another class of material connected with landownership which people usually find hard going when first confronted with them are manorial records, especially the proceedings of manor courts. Again, medieval court rolls, if they survive, will either have been published or will, frankly, be beyond most amateurs, but it is not always appreciated that manorial land tenure ('copyhold' or 'customaryhold') survived until 1925 and in some parts of the country remained widely used. The tenure was called copyhold because the tenant's title to his holding was an extract from the manor court roll recording his admittance to the farm or other property, i.e. a copy of the roll. The alternative name arose because the property was held 'according to the custom of the manor'. Copyhold conveyances, i.e. brief extracts from court rolls recording the date of the conveyance and the names of the outgoing and incoming tenants, turn up among the deeds to many properties; what is generally more valuable is the survival down to modern times of the complete rolls (usually in fact bound volumes by the eighteenth century) for the manor, in which all such conveyances are listed in chronological order. In parishes where most of the land remained copyhold or customaryhold until 1925 (instead of being converted to leasehold, tenancies at will or freehold), a long run of court books amounts to a miniature land registry for the parish. Here again, as with other bulky, repetitive sources, it may be helpful to note the details of each conveyance on slips or a computer database so that they can then be sorted by party and by holding to follow either the history of a particular farm or the career of a particular tenant. Even if most of an estate was held on non-manorial tenures, court rolls may still be a valuable source for the history of a few tenements which remain copyhold, possibly over a period of two or three centuries.

The registering of property transfers was the function of the 'court baron', whereas the 'court leet' was a meeting of local farmers at which rules for the management of the common fields and meadows were drawn up, and problems such as blocked ditches or encroachments on the common dealt with. Although technically separate, the two courts usually sat together before the same jury. In lowland areas leet business generally disappeared at the time of parliamentary inclosure, although some courts continued to nominate petty constables; in some upland areas the presence of large tracts of unenclosed moorland meant that courts still met to control the grazing of animals on the waste until modern commoners' associations took over that function.

Manor court records, like those of all courts, were kept in Latin until 1734 but later material should present no more problems than any other type of deed. Another technical problem which affects many early modern sources besides deeds is the practice of dating according to 'regnal years', rather than the ordinary calendar, e.g. 2 March, 12 Geo. III, meaning 2 March 1772. There is a standard manual from which one can solve this and other problems of chronology, such as the practice in medieval deeds of dating events according to saints' days. This virtually died out in England at the Reformation, except for the survival of Lady Day (25 March) and Michaelmas (29 September) as favoured dates for the start of leases and payment of rent.

Another point to remember is that until 1752 New Year's Day was reckoned to be 25 March, rather than 1 January, so that for most of the first three months of the year contemporaries dated documents a year earlier than that to which modern practice would assign them. Thus a document dated 15 January 1724 at the time it was written would be regarded as belonging to 1725 today. Sometimes this discrepancy is highlighted by writing '15 January 1724 old style' or '15 January 1725 new style'; another method is to give the date as '15 January 1724/5'.

Before listing deeds, archivists usually arrange them according to the property (or at least parish) to which they refer; if the collection has arrived at the office intact, it will often consist (at least in part) of bundles, one for each property. Within each bundle, deeds will usually be arranged chronologically, so that one can trace a succession of owners. If you are looking at deeds not in a record office (for example the deeds to your own house at the bank or building society), they will be easier to understand if you look at them in date order. Apart from anything else, it may become obvious that the description of the property was copied from one to the next without revision. Thus, 'all that newly erected messuage, tenement or dwelling house' (i.e. just a house) mentioned in 1850 may actually have been built in 1750, when the same phrase occurs for the first time. Interesting details such as 'now wholly or partly occupied by an iron furnace lately erected thereon' may be copied into deeds post-dating the demolition of the works; 'abutting westwardly on the lands of the Abbot of Welbeck' may occur in a deed of 1700 and be obviously wrong, but is useful evidence for the pre-1539 history of a neighbouring property.

The description of urban property in deeds before recent times is usually too imprecise to identify unless the deed is part of a bundle known to relate to a specific modern address: 'all that messuage ... in a road called St Mary's Gate' will only become 'all that property known as No 22 St Mary's Gate' about 1900 and, if the older deeds have become separated from modern conveyances, it may be difficult to re-unite them. In rural areas, named farms can normally be identified, especially in upland districts where a name applied to a single home-stead rather than a hamlet or village. Deeds merely conveying fields can sometimes be matched up with references to field-names on nineteenth-century maps. Deeds themselves tend not to have plans endorsed on them until the mid-nineteenth century, when first the tithe maps and later the 1:2500 Ordnance Survey became available.

There is one final short-cut to tracing the history of property from deeds which may help those put off by the size of the documents and the legal verbiage. On most bundles that are still intact there should be an 'Abstract of Title', drawn up by the vendor's solicitor when the property changed hands to show the purchaser that his client was entitled to sell the estate. Sometimes the abstract mentions deeds now lost; generally it will provide an adequate summary of each of the existing deeds. This may be worth having photocopied, because the abstract of each deed will be so concise as not to allow for much further shortening, whereas post-1700 original deeds are hardly ever worth copying. They are usually too big but, even if the record office is prepared to do them in several sections, you will merely find, after sticking the sheets together, that you have paid to have a lot of common form copied. It is useful to copy the plans found on modern deeds, which are often close to the edge of the document so that this can be done without damaging the parchment.

If you are trying to trace the history of an individual property, for example your own house or an ironworks or a cornmill, estate records, deeds and the maps described in the next chapter are the most useful sources for identifying specific properties and their owners or occupiers. They are also basic to a general study of landownership in a particular parish, whether it was a wholly rural community or a parish which became a suburb or mining village or a factory town, either in the nineteenth century or more recently. One or two other sources, which may be helpful in certain cases, may also be mentioned here.

Between 1780 and 1832 the clerk of the peace in each county kept duplicate copies of the land tax assessments for each township (the originals of which were sent up to the Exchequer in London), because only those who paid above a certain level were eligible to vote in parliamentary elections. Land tax was levied annually between 1692 and 1949 (when it was merged into income tax) but for most of that period all that survives (in the Public Record Office) are returns of the amount paid by each township, not each person. For this one important fifty-year period, however, during which there were major shifts in landownership in England and Wales as a result of agricultural and industrial change, detailed records are available locally in most counties; in a few cases material has also survived from before 1780 or after 1832. In principle, land tax assessments list for each township for every year the owners and occupiers of all the land and the amount of tax they paid thereon. In practice, there are a number of complications, on which a rather technical literature has grown up, but in simple terms land tax assessments are a very useful guide to 'who was who' in a particular community at the end of the eighteenth century and beginning of the nineteenth. They are especially valuable where there are no estate records, since they at least show who were the main owners, even if it proves impossible to relate the amount of tax paid to acreage owned or occupied. Very small occupiers often do not appear in the assessments or may be embraced under the formula 'Mr Smith and Others' which sometimes appears in the occupiers' columns, but otherwise they are a useful source.

Identifying individual houses in land tax assessments is not easy, even after the introduction of a column listing the 'premises' on which tax was paid, although in a small village where you know who was living at a particular house in, say, 1790, you may be able to follow its history through to 1830 by checking when the name changes in the list (the assessment was written out in the same order year after year). In towns this is usually impossible, as it is in any parish where little or no detail was entered in the premises column. Industrial buildings or houses of particular importance may be itemised from the start; for the cotton industry of the East Midlands, for example, where many small concerns had a fleeting, otherwise undocumented existence in the 1780s and 1790s, land tax assessments have been used to establish dates between which mills were in operation and by whom they were worked.

The collection of local rates, mainly in the second half of the eighteenth century and the early nineteenth, has sometimes left a legacy of ratebooks, which may be used in much the same way as land tax assessments. They are usually found in parish collections and typically consist of lists of people and the amount of rate paid (whichever rate it was—poor rate being the most common). If there is no topographical detail at all there is little hope of establishing more than the fact that John Smith was paying rates that year; if he is described as 'John Smith, for Townend Farm' that is more helpful. In towns where the ratebook was compiled by street and you can establish independently the names of one or two contemporary occupiers, you may be able to work out that the list is arranged systematically, starting at one end of the road and going along each side in turn, in which case you may be able to assign each ratepayer to a house. If you have a series of ratebooks extending as late as the mid nineteenth century, you may be able to use a census enumeration as a means of working out house-by-house occupancy in, say, 1851, and then work backwards through the ratebooks. One can also attempt a similar exercise using the tithe map of the 1840s and the land tax assessments from 1832 back to 1780, although this is time-consuming in a place of any size and difficult in a built-up area, where many occupiers tend not to be listed in either source.

As more of these detailed 'repopulation' exercises have been attempted in different parts of the country, one conclusion that has emerged is that, in many rural communities, houses were listed in much the same order for a variety of purposes over a very long period, so that hearth tax assessments, land tax assessments, ratebooks and even early census enumerations all follow a similar route. This will not have been the case everywhere, but it does appear that by collating a variety of sources one can extract more information about individual properties from those containing little or no topographical detail (such as hearth tax assessments) than used to be thought possible.

For the later nineteenth century ratebooks become so bulky, and so much of the information derived from them about individuals is available elsewhere, that many record offices only keep a sample for each parish—usually the census years (1841, 1851 etc.), so that they can be used in conjunction with enumerators' books (p. 35) to locate individuals and particular houses. More generally, ratebooks of this period are one source (the other main one being Ordnance Survey maps, see pp. 83-9) through which the growth of suburbs and new streets in expanding towns may be traced by checking a succession of books in order to pick up the first appearance of a street or estate.

People

The previous section explained what sources in a local record office are likely to be most useful in tracing the history of landownership or the history of a single house. The same documents, of course, like those created by local administration, also mention people, and anyone trying to trace a particular family or individual will find most of them useful for this purpose as well. In an office which has had the chance to list and index its deposited collections in depth, and possibly some of its official and diocesan material also, a search of the personal names index for a particular person or family is always worthwhile and takes virtually no time. What does take time, and beyond a certain point is not usually worth the effort, is searching large, unlisted or unindexed collections on the off-chance of finding a reference to the person you are interested in. On the other hand, record offices contain a number of important classes of material specifically concerned with individuals which, while not often indexed by name, are worth searching either for a genealogical project or some more general enquiry. Here it is worth reflecting on the fact that almost all local history is concerned to some extent with people, as indeed are most local records. A bundle of deeds does not really tell you the 'history of your house', since most houses have no 'history' as such: it supplies the names of the people who owned and occupied that house. Similarly, nineteenth-century business records or the minute books of local authorities become much more interesting when you look behind the letter-books and resolutions at who was writing the letters and passing the resolutions. All local historians, not just genealogists, should know how to trace people in the past.

The basic sources for such research are so well known from their use by family historians as not to need detailed explanation here. Thus parish registers (and the 'bishop's transcripts' made each year for the archdeacon's visitation) are usually the best place in which to start looking for someone between about 1550 and 1830, once you know

which parish they lived in, or at least roughly where. Before the middle
of the sixteenth century you are much more heavily dependent on the
records of central government (Chapter 5) or records created by the
ownership of land, of which the latter remain useful down to modern
times.

The other standard genealogical source long used in conjunction
with parish registers is wills, plus, more recently, the inventory of the
deceased's personal estate (but not freehold property) that was filed
with a will, at least up to about 1750. Until 1858 probate of wills (and
the formal 'administration' of intestate estates where the next of kin did
not simply divide things up between them privately) came within the
jurisdiction of the church courts, whose records are now mostly in
county record offices. Because of the demand for them by genealogists
they are usually well indexed by person, less well by place and
sometimes not at all by occupation. A similar demand has ensured that
accurate, up-to-date guides are available to probate material. The
lowest church official who had probate jurisdiction was normally the
archdeacon, in whose court wills of people with property in only one
place would generally be proved. Somewhat larger estates still confined
to a single diocese would be dealt with in the bishop's court; in most of
Wales and in some English dioceses wills were all proved in the
diocesan rather than an archdeaconry court. Finally, there was the
prerogative jurisdiction of the two archbishops of York and Canterbury
(of whom the latter had ultimate jurisdiction over the whole country),
in whose courts were proved the wills of people with property in more
than one diocese or those which were likely to prove contentious. The
records of the Prerogative Court of York are in the custody of the
Borthwick Institute of Historical Research at York University; those of
the Prerogative Court of Canterbury are available at the new Family
Records Centre established by the Public Record Office (pp. 150-1).
Other pre-1858 probate records are held locally, including most of
those for the various oddities in the system ('peculiars') which existed
before 1858. Most Welsh church records, including all the probate
material and some parish registers, are at the National Library at
Aberystwyth (pp. 158-9).

Once you have established which local court people from your
community, or the family in which you are interested, would have dealt
with in probate matters, it is usually fairly simply to check whether a
particular person left a will, or if letters of administration were taken

out for his estate. Wills, as genealogical textbooks have long told us, are invaluable in supplying the names of the children, nephews, nieces and so on of the testator and thus fitting together what may be unconnected references in the parish register. They are also much more personal in character than deeds or administrative records. If the original will taken to court by the executor has survived, it will also give an indication, from the quality of the handwriting and the presence or absence of a signature or 'mark', as to the literacy of the writer; alternatively, there may only be a copy of the will written into a contemporary will register, where the name at the end is not an autograph.

From the early sixteenth century to the mid eighteenth it was customary for an inventory to be made of the personal estate of anyone whose affairs came before the probate court, and for this to be 'exhibited' (not proved) by the executors when they presented the will for probate, or by administrators when they sought letters of administration. During the last forty years these documents, which for most parts of the country survive in great number, have become well known and many have been published. Because they are inventories of personal, not real, estate, they are not a complete measure of a deceased's wealth, but where they have been compiled room by room they give a fascinating picture of how someone's house was furnished, and the total valuation is obviously a rough guide to wealth and social standing. In rural communities few sources are so useful for the history of farming, as opposed to landownership, since detailed inventories will itemise crops, animals and implements. For the history of early modern towns, inventories are a basic source for establishing how people earned a living and what sort of capital was needed in different trades. Lists of creditors and debtors in both rural and urban inventories reveal how much small-scale money-lending went on in this period, and from what sort of area tradesmen bought raw materials or sold finished goods.

If you are interested in a specific person or family from the sixteenth century onwards (comparatively few medieval wills survive and no probate inventories in the later sense) check to see whether a will exists. Most people did not make wills and most families did not bother with the expense of taking out letters of administration, but where there is a will it will certainly be worth looking at (with any supporting documentation such as an inventory) and probably having copied. The handwriting of pre-1660 original wills (and most registered copies) is usually fairly difficult for the beginner but this is one source where the effort to read the hand is likely to be rewarded.

Probate records are equally valuable for the local historian studying a community as a whole. Especially in parishes which have no surviving estate material, wills and inventories will often be the largest single source of information before 1800. In a county where the wills have been indexed by place it is easy enough to find all the documents for your parish; where you have to search an unprinted name index looking for references to a parish it will take longer to identify all the relevant material. Even so, the value of probate records is such that it is worthwhile; it is also worth looking at all the documents filed for each testator. It is not the case that wills are useful for genealogists and inventories for local historians; this is a bogus distinction. For a detailed community study it is even worth going through the largely formal bonds surviving from grants of administration to the next of kin of those who died without leaving wills, since odd snippets of information about individuals will appear here which may not be found elsewhere.

In 1858 probate jurisdiction was transferred to a lay court which established a network of district registries not dissimilar from that of the diocesan courts which they replaced, as well as a principal registry in London. A major change, however, was that instead of each court keeping its own index to grants, a printed calendar was compiled annually for the whole of England and Wales, listing in one sequence all the wills proved throughout the country, irrespective of where the transaction took place (in the early years administrations were indexed in a separate sequence, but this was soon given up). This greatly simplifies the process of tracing a grant, especially since most of the index volumes (up to about 1950) are now available in some county record offices (generally on microfiche). They can also be consulted in London at the Family Records Centre or at the recently opened Probate Search Room (42-49 High Holborn, WC1), where you can also read copies of the will and obtain photocopies. The will registers kept at each local registry from 1858 are now at local record offices, although except where they have been microfilmed it is impracticable to make copies from the volumes. Civil wills, and indeed most wills since 1750, do not have inventories with them.

Just as probate jurisdiction was overhauled in the mid nineteenth century, so, some years before, was the registration of vital events. In 1837 compulsory registration by the state of birth and death was introduced into England and Wales, a far more thorough system than was ever achieved by relying on church registration of baptism and burial. In the case of marriage registration, the Church of England and, to a lesser extent, the other denominations were taken into partnership with the state, so that all marriages were recorded in civil registers, and a duplicate record was kept of church weddings. This system of registration has not changed very much since 1837 and its working is well known. At the centre, the Registrar General is now an official within the Office for National Statistics and the indexes to births, marriages and deaths throughout England and Wales, which for some years were made available at St Catherine's House in the Aldwych, are now at the Family Records Centre. They have also been published on microfiche and so are available in some local libraries and record offices.

Searches for birth, marriage and death certificates can be made at the offices of a local superintendent registrar, if you know fairly precisely when and where a particular event took place, although in many cases enquiries to local offices are tiresome for both the searcher and the office, given the limited means of reference available and the pressure on local registrars from those wishing to register new events. As is well known, information from registers can only be supplied in the form of fairly expensive copy certificates. For those who enjoy participating in what is probably the last of the Whig administrative reforms of the 1830s to survive almost unchanged, using the local registration service for historical research has a certain period charm; for others, however, including many who work in the service, the time for major reform (involving the transfer of the older registers to archival custody) is long overdue.

Birth, marriage and death certificates, like post-1858 wills, are not merely the staple fare of genealogists; they can be useful for far more general enquiries. The history of a house, an estate or a business may turn on family relationships as revealed by a comparatively modern will or marriage. It is unusual for a genealogist not to be able to trace a moderately well-off family back to about 1800, through registration certificates and probate grants, and the same process in reverse is sometimes worth pursuing (for rather different motives) by a local historian. Not all family, business and estate papers are in record offices, and if you are interested in say, a small estate wound up about 1920, or a business that closed in the 1950s, it may be worth tracing the present whereabouts of the family concerned, using ordinary genealogical sources (plus such obvious material as the telephone directory, *Who's Who* and electors' lists) to ask if anything survives in their possession. If documents do turn up, it is then best to ask the local record office to try to secure them on deposit, or take copies, rather than make an offer to the owner yourself.

So far this section has been concerned with tracing people in general in archival sources, who can of course also be found in printed material in libraries. Another source of this kind which is available in county record offices and, for more recent periods, in local libraries, is registers of electors for each borough and county from 1832 to the present. Before 1867, and in country districts until 1884, the franchise remained restricted to men of a certain wealth; nineteenth-century electoral registers are therefore by no means a complete list of residents, or even householders, but they are still useful in locating individuals once one knows roughly where they were living at a particular time. They are arranged topographically, rather than alphabetically, so that to make a complete search of a large town for one person is hardly realistic. Conversely, once full addresses for urban property emerge, it is easy enough to establish who was living at a particular house in a given year, and in country parishes with individually named farms this is possible from an earlier date.

County record offices also have several classes of material which are useful for tracing individuals engaged in specific activities, particularly criminal or socially undesirable ones such as being poor. Today, most criminal offences are tried before magistrates in courts that are the successors to petty sessions, which were so called to distinguish them from the grander courts of quarter sessions, meetings of (in theory) all the magistrates for a county or large borough. Modem magistrates' court records less than 30 years old are not available for inspection and those of petty sessions are not well preserved, since the proceedings, before one or two magistrates resident in a locality, were relatively informal. The criminal records of quarter sessions, however, are for most counties reasonably complete from 1800 if not earlier; they are a good source for the history of crime which was too serious to be dealt with in petty sessions but which did not on the other hand reach the assize courts in England (whose records are at the PRO) or the court of great sessions in Wales (whose records are at the National Library). As well as providing the raw material for general studies of crime in the localities, quarter sessions material can be used by local historians interested in a particular place who are prepared to search fairly voluminous material for references to their own locality. This is obviously more likely to yield results in a town, as opposed to a rural parish with fewer inhabitants where a local resident magistrate kept order and hardly any matters went to quarter sessions.

Although the poor undoubtedly leave less behind them in the past than the rich, one well known local source for their study is the examinations and removal orders executed by magistrates enforcing the pre-1834 poor law, assisted by the overseers of the poor in each township. If the overseers encountered a stranger who might become a charge on the parish because of age, poverty, pregnancy or infirmity they normally presented them to the nearest magistrate. The justice would extract from the stranger the name of their home parish, or at least a place where they have previously lived long enough to gain a legal 'settlement' and entitlement to poor relief. If they could not prove that they were entitled to legal settlement in the place into which they had come, the magistrate would sign a removal order addressed to the overseers: this required them to convey the unfortunate victim to the first parish along the road toward that in which they had settlement, however far that might be. The removal orders may have ended up either in quarter sessions records or with the overseers' accounts in parish collections; examinations are usually in the latter. They do not survive for all parishes and some places—for example villages in the Midlands astride Watling Street will have more than a remote township in the West Country—but some record offices have compiled a consolidated index of personal and place-names from settlement papers, however these have reached the office. Like quarter sessions material, this source can be used to study poverty in a particular county, to trace ancestors who fell on hard times, or to add to the overall picture of life in your community in the seventeenth and eighteenth centuries. Removal orders are largely formal but examinations contain much human detail of movement from place to place in search of work.

Industry, transport and trade

A number of printed sources for the local history of industry and transport, especially nineteenth-century directories, were mentioned in Chapter 2; this is also an area well served by secondary material, including the voluminous literature of railway history, the newer but now quite extensive bibliography of canal history, books on road transport and road vehicles, and the vast quantity of books and pamphlets which has marked the rise of industrial archaeology since the 1960s. There are also innumerable published histories—good, bad and indifferent—of individual businesses. Local historians interested either in transport generally in their chosen area, or in local industry, should be able to find a fair amount of information from such sources. Archival material available locally, or indeed anywhere, especially for small-scale industry or minor transport undertakings, may be more limited.

If you wish to pursue the history of a particular firm, or an industry made up of several businesses, the best way to start is almost always to compile lists of names from successive directories (p. 29). If it is an industry carried out in fairly extensive premises which can be identified on large-scale maps (Chapter 4) each of the firms can then be located on the ground, where it is always worth checking whether buildings survive. Workshop or cottage industries, such as nail making or stocking knitting, are obviously harder to trace in this way. Industries with a strong 'territorial' character, such as coal mining or iron and steel manufacture, should certainly be studied topographically, together with associated railways, tramways or branch canals, and industrial housing. Once you have worked out the dates between which a business operated, or located on the ground the site of an ironworks, watermill or whatever, it is worth turning to the resources of the local record office.

Since only in a few cases will business records survive, it is best to think of how else one can reconstruct the history of an enterprise. Several pieces of advice have been offered on earlier pages: identify the parish in which the business operated and see what is available generally in the way of unprinted maps or estate records, the latter possibly including leases by a ground landlord whose muniments have survived where his lessees' papers have not (p. 59); search land tax assessments (p. 67) to try to establish dates of operation in the period prior to that in which directories become available, and also note the occupiers' names; check the personal names index for all the names you have culled from directories and other sources in case stray deeds (including partnership deeds) have come into the office; try the main genealogical sources (the census, parish registers and wills) to build up biographical details of the owners.

The approach to avoid is that of merely asking the archivist for any business papers from the firm of Bloggs & Co., dyers and bleachers of No Mans Heath, 1860-1900, since you will almost certainly be told, on the basis of a brief search of the indexes, that there are none in the office. What there will be, however, will be maps marking Messrs Bloggs's premises, which were perhaps converted from an earlier water cornmill belonging to a local estate, whose muniments may include a bundle listed as 'No Mans Heath Mill, leases, 1750-1860'. These might identify half a dozen previous occupiers of the site and possibly mention other industries which used the mill before it became a bleachworks. If the last directory to name the works identifies the owner as Bloggs & Jones, try the record office index under the other name. Possibly Mr Jones's solicitor, who wound up the business when Bloggs died, has deposited material which includes probate or bankruptcy papers. None of this comes under the heading of 'business records' strictly speaking, but it is far more typical of what is to be found for most companies in a record office than is sometimes suggested in the more optimistic textbooks. Few eighteenth- or nineteenth-century businesses have not left some trace in local records but for even fewer will a record office have any but fragmentary internal records.

A major source for business history, especially between about 1870 and the First World War and to some extent for earlier and later periods, still little used by local historians, is the series of 'Files of Dissolved Companies' transferred from Companies House to the Public Record Office and therefore described in Chapter 6 (p. 147).

If you are fortunate, you may find that for perhaps one business in the town, or one representative of a once widespread local industry, a good set of records has been deposited or, more commonly, rescued by an alert archivist. Apart from deeds, which may included both convey-ances of the premises occupied by the business and deeds establishing or dissolving the formal co-partnerships through which most companies operated before limited liability became general, accounting records are probably the most likely to have survived. There may be sales ledgers, with an account for each customer, in which hopefully goods will have been entered as '200 tramplates, 45^{lb} p^r yard, marked G.J. CANAL C^{OY}.', not merely as 'Goods'. Or there may be a partnership ledger, setting out how the original share capital was raised, what dividends were paid, what was done when the first partners died, and how the nominal value of the firm grew. The other most common survival tends to be correspondence, either letters received by the firm or copies of outgoing letters. Whether loose, in bundles or in letter-books the most interesting of these will probably be enquiries about products or estimates supplied to prospective customers. In a large collection a great many of the out-letters may prove on examination to be chasing unpaid accounts or dealing with other routine matters.

The archive material for two of the major nineteenth-century industrial staples in which local historians are often interested should perhaps be mentioned separately. Early colliery records, up to the middle of the nineteenth century, are scarce outside the North Eastern coalfield, which was by far the largest producer in this period. Elsewhere the typical unit of production was too small to generate much in the way of records, and maps and leases in estate collections are often the only sources. More modern company records were vested in the National Coal Board in 1947, which subsequently deposited most of the material in appropriate county record offices. On the other hand a great deal was destroyed by the private owners on the eve of nationalisation, as folk-memory in every coalfield will testify. A multi-volume history of the industry, commissioned by the NCB in happier days, provides, in the bibliographies printed in each volume as well as a separately published compilation, an invaluable guide to both published and unpublished sources for the local history of coalmining. British Coal retained, until its demise, large quantities of colliery plans (both surface and underground) and engineering drawings, some of which have since been distributed to local record offices, while others are in the hands of the successor Coal Authority. Plans of abandoned collieries are kept by the Health and Safety Executive at Bootle (whereas those of other types of mine have been dispersed to local record offices).

For the iron (and later steel) industry, there are several major collections for the eighteenth century preserved among the muniments of families who controlled the large partnerships which dominated the industry in this period, and some earlier material, especially for the Weald and parts of the West Midlands. For the Industrial Revolution period, however, between about 1780 and 1870, far fewer business records survive and most have probably now been used for published company histories. Later material generally passed into the hands of British Steel, which is gradually transferring pre-1967 records of the former private companies from its own records centres to local record offices. The company has sadly not followed the example of the NCB in sponsoring a definitive general history of the industry, although there is an excellent guide to archival sources published by the Historical Manuscripts Commission.

If such major industries as coal and iron are often poorly documented at the level of the individual firm, it may be appreciated how little can usually be found for the typical local business. Approaches to surviving old established firms direct are generally unproductive, unless one has some personal contact. Either the letter is not answered or the company say nothing has survived. This may be true, although in years gone by it was often the case that some long-serving employee was guarding material for his forthcoming centenary history and did not want anyone else to see it. Today, however, when all the older heavy industries, once dominated by large companies that did create extensive archives, have undergone such radical changes, the chances of finding a strong-room in an empty office full of documents everyone in the firm had long forgotten about are far less likely than they were a generation ago.

The archives of local retailing or wholesaling are generally non-existent, and anyone interested in the history of shopping will usually be dependent on directories, old newspapers and the like, which together can yield quite a full account of the period from about 1830. For a much earlier period, urban inventories often include good examples relating to shopkeepers, especially mercers and drapers. Directories are usually the only source available for the local history of carrying and coach services; they are also a good starting point for a perennially popular project: tracing the history of inns in a town. For the fifty years or so prior to the start of detailed local directories it is worth looking at 'alehouse recognisances', a category of quarter sessions record, which supply the names of licensees and those who stood surety for them for good behaviour before the licensing justices each year. By the 1810s and 1820s the name of the pub is sometimes also given. Again, for the earlier history of inns, inventories are an unrivalled source, although the pubs are rarely named.

For the history of roads themselves there are several sources in local record offices, although these have often been pretty thoroughly worked over and it may be possible to rely on secondary material. Today, most roads are maintained by county councils, whose responsibility dates from 1889, when it was handed over by the justices. Quarter sessions exercised mainly a supervisory role in the earlier period, the actual maintenance being the job, usually ill-executed, of the parish surveyors until 1835, thereafter of district highway boards. From the early eighteenth century many main roads were taken out of the hands of the parish and maintained by turnpike trusts established for the purpose, which, under the authority of an Act of Parliament, repaired and sometimes built stretches of road, borrowed money to do so, and attempted to repay the money by charging tolls for the use of the improved roads. The trusts became hopelessly insolvent with the coming of the railways and were eventually rescued by the county councils, who thus acquired many of their records, which may include minutes and accounts. The counties have been directly responsible for bridges on main roads (i.e. 'county bridges') for much longer and quarter sessions records should contain papers from the county surveyor for at least the nineteenth century, if not earlier. Thus if your community has a fine eighteenth-century bridge carrying a main road over a river, the chances are that details of its construction (including the cost and the name of the architect responsible) can be traced from this source.

The improvement of river navigation between about 1660 and 1760 took much the same institutional form as the turnpiking of roads, with a body of commissioners acting under the authority of a local Act. When canals were built in the later eighteenth century and early nineteenth somewhat different Acts were obtained incorporating shareholders into a company which owned the canal and associated works outright. This type of corporation was also adopted by the promoters of the more ambitious pre-locomotive railway schemes of the period 1800-30, and subsequently followed by the early main line railway companies of the next fifteen years, which evolved into the large national concerns of the later nineteenth century.

When the railways, most of the canals, the larger docks and much of the road transport industry were brought into public ownership after the Second World War, the British Transport Commission set up two record offices to house its archives centrally. This collection is now at the Public Record Office (p. 133), although a good deal of material relating to the civil and mechanical engineering aspects of the railways, including huge numbers of photographs, is at the National Railway Museum at York, and for canals there is also the National Waterways Museum at Gloucester, as well as the older established British Water-ways museum at Stoke Bruerne (Northants.). Both the railway and canal records at Kew, and the collections at York, have been heavily used for published histories, so that for most undertakings there will usually be several articles, if not a full-length book, in the local library.

The recent return of the railways to private ownership has created serious archival problems. Not only has Railtrack retained a considerable quantity of civil engineering records of great historical interest, but the train operating companies and other successors to British Rail are generating a large volume of administrative and financial records, comparable in importance to those at Kew for the period before 1947, for which no arrangements have yet been made for custody and access once they cease to be required for administrative use.

Since most railway, canal and dock company archives are held centrally there is limited scope for the use of primary material by local historians without ready access to the PRO or NRM. The one source that will be in the local record office, although it has uses beyond the field of transport history, is the plan deposited with the clerk of the peace in advance of an application to parliament for authority to build a canal, railway or other project, whether or not the scheme went ahead (pp. 106-7).

The modern history of road transport has a somewhat smaller enthusiast following than railways, but for anyone interested in the tram, trolley-bus and motor-bus undertakings of local authorities there should be minutes (and possibly other material) of the appropriate committee among the records of the borough or urban district council concerned. Business records of private road transport operators are very scarce, although it may be worth using the motor vehicle registration records kept by county and county borough councils between 1904 and 1974, of which a fair proportion have survived to reach county record offices, to identify early vehicles. The same source can also be used for the early history of private car ownership in a community.

Conclusion

This chapter is the longest in the book and has tried to summarise what is available (or not) in most county record offices for some of the topics most often pursued by local historians. It does not seek to provide a comprehensive guide to the contents of local offices or go into as much detail as more specialised guides to particular sources, of which a number are listed under Further Reading. Many of these are aimed at family historians, although I have tried to suggest here that much of this material has a wider value. Readers with a general interest in their (preferably fairly small) community should find something of value in each section of the chapter; those who merely want to trace the history of the brickworks at the end of their garden may pick up some hints but will soon have to turn to books specifically concerned with brick-making. However wide or narrow your research project, one thing is certain: that in addition to using the printed sources outlined in the previous chapter and the archive material described here, you will also wish to use maps, both new and old, and indeed may well have started by looking at whatever you are interested in on a map. Since they are so basic to local history and are to be found in both libraries and record offices, a separate chapter has been allotted to them, which amplifies the passing references in this and the previous chapter.

CHAPTER FOUR

Maps

All modern books on local history dwell heavily on the importance of maps, both those published by the Ordnance Survey and earlier unprinted material, especially those drawn up for tithe or inclosure awards. This is usually coupled with a similar stress on the landscape itself, as portrayed in maps and visible on the ground. There is a long tradition of interest among English antiquaries in the value of field evidence, which was one of the aspects of the subject urged most strongly by the Leicester School, especially Hoskins himself, in the post-war renaissance of local history, and his ideas, pathbreaking in their day, are now commonplace. Most of those who become interested in local history need little reminder of the value of landscape evidence, since they tend to be the sort of people who already go for walks in the country, visit historic houses and join the National Trust. Furthermore, the first sources many local historians look at are maps, particularly those fairly readily available in public libraries. This chapter has the twin aims of setting out what map sources are available, either for the whole country or particular parishes, and how they can be used to recreate past landscapes. The chapter following considers the use of physical evidence itself, whether from archaeological evidence, fieldwork or the surveying of old buildings.

Ordnance Survey maps

Great Britain has the good fortune to be the best mapped country on Earth, thanks to the work of the world's finest mapmaking organisation, the Ordnance Survey. All local historians will be familiar with its best known publication, the 1:50,000 map of the whole country, which replaced the earlier one-inch to the mile (1:63,360) survey more than twenty years ago. Useful though the sheets of the 1:50,000 survey are for coverage of a fairly large region, an essential investment for the local historian interested in a small area are the relevant sheets of the 1:25,000 map (roughly two and a half inches to the mile). This was first issued shortly after the Second World War in a provisional edition, using pre-war material, to provide a new folding map intermediate in scale between the one-inch and six-inch series. It is now published in a much more attractive format, with greater use of colour, drawing on up-to-date survey data, and is indispensable for any kind of field exploration. Although it does not help greatly with the study of particular sites, the 1:25,000 map is invaluable as a readily portable map on a scale on which it is possible to mark field boundaries as well as buildings, roads, railways and natural features.

The original 1:25,000 map was created by reducing older sheets of what was then the six-inch to the mile survey (1:10,560), which was rescaled some years ago as 1:10,000. This is published for all but the most remote parts of the country and, together with its larger brother, the 1:2500 map (which has always been published on a metric scale but is colloquially known as the '25-inch map'), is the OS series with the longest history after the one-inch survey.

The Ordnance Survey was established in 1791 to prepare up-to-date maps of the counties of south-east England—Kent, Surrey and Sussex—as a preparation for repelling possible French invaders. After the war ended in 1815 the survey work of the Board of Ordnance was continued and gradually extended to the rest of the country. The original maps were published on a scale which had already become well established in the eighteenth century for privately produced county maps (p. 90), one inch to the mile, although the OS sheets formed a continuous set for the whole country, unlike their predecessors. The 'Old Series' of the one-inch map was not completed until about 1870, by which time many sheets had become badly out of date as towns expanded, railways were built and the English landscape changed more drastically than it had for centuries. No systematic revision was carried out on the old series (for which the term 'First Edition' implies a neatness in publication which was not the case), apart from the addition of railway lines and a few other features. Although the OS did not fall into the trap of some private mapmakers of inserting projected railways, many of which were never built, they did continue to issue sheets revised to show railways which still bore the original date of publication. Apart from establishing when the railways in question were opened, there is virtually no way of working out when such sheets were published, or whether any other details were changed.

Most local studies libraries and record offices have copies of the old series one-inch map for their area. Especially where the sheets have been trimmed and mounted, thus removing any dates at all, it is difficult to discover when the sheet was surveyed, particularly if it was one of those where there was a long delay between survey and publication. Some years ago David & Charles produced facsimile reprints of the old series maps for the whole country, issued in either a folded format similar to modern OS maps or as flat sheets, most of which are still available. These have some value in making the maps accessible in a convenient format, but the standard of reproduction was variable and the sheets used for the reprints ranged widely over the period in which the old series was published. In some cases, composite maps were made up from the quarter-sheets in which certain areas were originally published; where different quarters are from different printings the new edition may have railway lines stopping half-way across the sheet. A marginal commentary explained some of these difficulties but the project fell short of a scholarly facsimile edition. A few years later Harry Margary published a series closer to this ideal but the maps were issued in volumes and were much more expensive, so that they are mainly to be found in academic libraries and private collections. The underlying problem with any scheme of this kind is that there is no complete set of what can properly be called a 'first edition' of the one-inch map. The Ordnance Survey's own records suffered badly in the Second World War and neither the British Library nor the Bodleian has complete holdings (Cambridge University and the other national libraries did not then have a copyright privilege which extended to maps).

The old series one-inch maps are of some use for the study of local topography, coming mid-way between the privately produced maps of the late eighteenth century and the second edition of the as, but the scale is too small to do more than identify the existence or absence of certain fairly obvious features. Tracing tramroads in mining areas is a good example of a project for which the old series OS can be useful; the gradual spread of suburbs over the period 1830-70 is a subject on which they are highly unreliable.

Local historians making a detailed study of their area will probably wish to supplement a photocopy of the first one-inch map with a copy of the earlier drawing from which it was engraved, which is on a scale of two inches to the mile and may contain details omitted from the published map. The original drawings were destroyed during the Second World War but photographs had previously been made for the

British Museum, from which the British Library Map Room can supply copies; for Wales there is a set of prints at the National Library.

By the middle of the nineteenth century it was clear that the work of the Ordnance Survey needed overhauling. The department had already done some surveying intended for publication on a much larger scale than 1:63,360, for example in Ireland and the West Riding, and in the 1870s began the publication, following closely on survey in most areas, of a completely new 'second edition', which marks the start of modern OS publishing. A policy of concentrating on three scales was established, which has lasted to the present. The one-inch map was issued in folding sheets with some use of colour, and thus became popular with the growing numbers who wished to explore the countryside on foot or, later, bicycle, an activity which became easier as the railway network was extended. For those who wanted a larger scale, which included some ordinary purchasers but mainly meant landowners, local authorities and public utilities, the survey was published (except in mountainous areas) at what then seemed a logical scale of six inches to the mile (1:10,560). Finally, for those who needed a large-scale plan of either built-up or rural areas, the 25-inch map (1:2500) was produced.

While the second (and later) editions of the one-inch map are of little interest to local historians, the publication of the first six-inch and 25-inch maps marks the beginning of the period in which one can trace the micro-topography of almost anywhere. Both the larger scales are useful in different ways. If you are interested in a particular feature, such as a country house, cotton mill, colliery, ironworks or railway station, the 25-inch sheets are indispensable. The scale is sufficiently generous to mark standard gauge railway lines to the correct width (which the smaller scales do not) and show not merely the existence but the shape of all but the smallest buildings. At an ironworks you should be able to count the number of blast furnaces; at a country house you can see if the conservatory was there. Boundaries of fields and other parcels of land are shown, with the acreage given for all but small private house-plots. Because of their aesthetic as well as cartographical appeal (especially the hand coloured versions), the first edition 1:2500 maps are a marvellous source for bringing alive the landscape of the 1870s and 1880s.

The first edition of the six-inch map, although obviously less detailed than the 25-inch and visually less appealing, nonetheless has its uses. For one thing, a photocopy covering an entire parish (except in upland areas with very large parishes) remains a manageable size, which is rarely the case with the larger scale. Secondly, if you are interested in the evolution of a complete landscape, such as a parish, a copy from the six-inch map gives you an overall picture of the extent of building, the existence of parks and woodland, industrial features and so on, which small extracts from a 25-inch sheet do not. Thirdly, the six-inch map is often a better base on which to mark up features from earlier maps (see below), unless you are concerned with a very small area.

Whether you are interested in a whole landscape or only one feature therein, an obvious step in any topographical project is to get a photocopy of each six-inch or 25-inch map from *c*. 1880 onwards. There was an initial revision of the two larger scales around 1900 and another about 1920; for some areas there was a somewhat inadequately revised fourth edition just before the Second World War. Since 1945 there has been a process of continuous revision of the larger scales, as well as a complete rearrangement of sheet lines following the introduction of the National Grid. The grid will be familiar to new users of the large-scale maps from its appearance on the 1:50,000 and 1:25,000 sheets, which all contain an explanation of how the system works, but it is worth noting that the grid also forms a reference system to modern 1:10,000 and 1:2500 sheets. A six-inch or 1:10,000 map published since the introduction of the National Grid is numbered using the letters and figures which identify the 10 km. square covered by the sheet, while the 1:2500 sheets have four-digit numbers identifying a 1 km. square. Before the Second World War, both series were numbered in a separate sequence for each county. The six-inch sheets had Roman numerals, to which was added an arabic number to identify the one-sixteenth portion of each sheet covered by a 1:2500 map. Thus a six-inch map of the extreme north-west corner of Barsetshire would be Barsetshire I, and the 25-inch sheet covering the south-easternmost corner of the same six-inch map would be Barsetshire I.16. When this system was current the OS published an index sheet for each county, showing where the sheet lines fell and all libraries and record offices with map collections for their area keep a copy of this index to hand for readers to identify the sheet they wish to see, sometimes marked-up to indicate which editions of each map they have in stock.

Crown copyright in Ordnance Survey maps lasts for fifty years from the date of publication, after which they may be copied freely. To supply copies of more recent maps, a library or record office must have a licence from the OS, whose copyright branch operates with a ferocity so notorious as to make the unauthorised copying of current maps distinctly unwise. The OS themselves supply the large-scale maps as prints made from negatives supplied to trade agents which, although still expensive, are cheaper than conventionally printed sheets and allow for the rapid incorporation of new survey data.

A technical rather than legal problem in copying old OS maps is that on small office machines that only make copies up to A3 size it is possible to tear fragile sheet maps, and this has made some libraries and record offices reluctant to make cheap copies. They may insist that copies can only be made photographically, which is expensive and almost impossible to do precisely to scale, or by tracing, which is tedious and also rarely produces very accurate results. Few (if any) local libraries or record offices have large-format plan printers, which will make copies up to A0 size with no damage to flat originals, although equipment of this sort is available in most towns at specialist copy shops catering for architects and surveyors. If you are undertaking a serious piece of topographical research for which a complete sequence of high quality, true-scale copies of a number of maps is more or less essential, it may be worth suggesting to a sympathetic librarian or archivist that the maps in question be allowed out to be copied by such a firm, perhaps offering to make an extra copy for the library itself to save wear and tear on their own originals in the future. If this fails, it is worth approaching the British Library Map Room, which can supply superb, if rather expensive, copies from their collection covering the whole country; for Wales the National Library's Department of Pictures and Maps offers a similar service at a much lower price.

For a local historian working on a rural landscape, or a coalfield area, a sequence of six-inch or 25-inch maps will give a clear picture of the how the area has changed over the last century. If you are working on a town or looking at the growth of suburbs there are other Ordnance Survey plans that provide an even fuller picture. One of these is the current 50-inch (1:1250) survey of built-up areas, of which each sheet covers a quarter of the area of a 25-inch map. This was introduced after the Second World War to provide a better base in towns where the 1:2500 map was becoming congested. There are no older editions on this scale, except a one-off set of plans produced for the Inland Revenue around 1910 in connection with land valuation, which are merely mechanical enlargements of the 1900 edition of the 1:2500 map with no additional detail.

In the 1870s, as part of the second edition survey, the OS published a magnificent series of town plans on various scales around 1:500 (the 'ten-foot scale'), which are arguably the finest maps they have ever produced. For anyone interested in a town covered on this scale they are invaluable, coming before slum clearance or other late nineteenth-century changes began. Not merely is every parcel boundary and every house shown, but for public buildings there are interior plans and a note of the seating capacity; street furniture is shown to scale, and there is far more legend than on the 25-inch sheets. Railway and industrial installations are also shown in fascinating detail. This exercise was never repeated (although for a few towns the local authority financed a revised edition around the turn of the century) but a generation earlier the OS were engaged by the newly established General Board of Health to produce surveys for towns where the 1848 Public Health Act was adopted and a local board of health set up (pp. 54, 146). Here again superb large-scale plans were prepared; indeed, one of the criticisms of the Board of Health was that it commissioned unnecessarily detailed surveys (also on a scale of around 10ft to the mile) merely to identify problems of poor housing and inadequate drainage, which delayed remedial action and added to the cost of adopting the Act. For those towns included in these surveys, however, they are another excellent source for urban topography, which can be compared with the plans of the 1870s and possibly used for 'house repopulation' in conjunction with the 1851 census, just as the later plans can be linked to the enumerators' books of 1871 or 1881 (p. 39).

This section has outlined those resources of the Ordnance Survey which the beginner is likely to make use of. For more advanced work the OS, which is at the forefront of research into the electronic handling of cartographic data, has various specialist services which may be of interest, and has some archival material, relating for example to boundaries and land utilisation, which is divided between its own headquarters and the Public Record Office. There is a growing technical literature on early OS maps and a specialist society (the Charles Close Society, named after the first director-general) devoted to the agency's history.

Other printed maps

In the half-century before the Ordnance Survey was established virtually every English county, and some in Wales, were equipped with a privately produced map similar in style to those later issued by the OS. In particular, most were published on a scale of one inch to the mile which remained the standard for medium-scale British maps for another two centuries. The difference between the early OS maps and their immediate predecessors is that the latter were mostly maps of a single county, rather than a continuous stretch of country, and obviously do not join together to provide complete or consistent coverage of the whole country. They also vary in the accuracy and detail of the surveying and, to some extent, in the conventional signs used. In the 1820s two brothers, Christopher and John Greenwood, set out to publish a uniform set of one-inch county maps for the whole of England, a project which marks the climax of seventy years of private mapmaking on this scale. By this date, however, the Ordnance Survey was well on its way to covering the whole country and the abandonment of the Greenwoods' venture effectively marks the end of competition of this sort.

The privately produced county maps, the work of a small group of surveyors, several of whom published maps for more than one county, provide much the same level of detail as the early one-inch OS maps. Only the limited number published on a two-inch scale claim to show every field (and then with questionable accuracy) but even on the smaller scale it was possible, in the relatively uncrowded landscape of the late eighteenth century, to mark wind- and water-mills (the latter usually with a small asterisk-like symbol) and other industrial features, turnpike roads, canals, country houses and parks. A useful convention not adopted by the OS was the inclusion of the landowner's name alongside his mansion, since these were the people whom the surveyor hoped would buy what were always very expensive publications.

A number of county maps included an inset plan on a larger scale of the county town, and towns generally tend to be better mapped than country areas before the coming of the large-scale Ordnance Survey in the 1870s. London has a long sequence of commercially produced plans and most of the larger provincial towns have at least one eighteenth century street plan. After 1800 such maps become common for quite small places, either separately published or included in town histories or directories. There was also a practice in this period, for both London and the main provincial centres, of publishing one-inch or larger scale maps of the country twenty, thirty or more miles around a particular place, which are similar in style to contemporary county maps. From the mid nineteenth century commercially published town plans tend to be derived simply from OS data and thus contain nothing of particular interest.

There is one later series that is worth mentioning, the large-scale coloured plans published by Charles E. Goad from the 1880s onwards which were based on the Ordnance Survey but with additional detail indicating the use to which commercial premises were put, the materials from which buildings were constructed, and other information of interest to the intended users of such maps—the fire insurance industry—such as the storage of inflammable materials or the presence of a steam engine or other motive power. For the detailed study of industry and commerce in built-up areas these maps are invaluable and are fairly widely available in local libraries (copies can also be obtained from the British Library). Goad revised the series by issuing sheets containing new material relating to particular buildings or streets, which had to be cut out and pasted on to the original maps, the results of which can often be seen on copies that have been updated by users. Revisions (and new printings of complete maps) continued to be published until after the Second World War; as demand from the insurance industry for this rather specialised product declined, Goad switched to producing town plans identifying the occupiers and usage of retail premises, which were aimed at developers and prospective tenants. These maps, of which the older printings are themselves now of historical value, continue to be published.

Both the one-inch county maps and early town plans have been widely reprinted in recent years, sometimes with an analytical introduction. These facsimiles are invaluable in making available, usually quite cheaply, an immensely useful and also visually appealing source for both urban and rural topography, which previously could only be traced, photographed or subjected to ill-treatment on early photocopiers.

Also widely available as cheap reprints, but of decorative rather than practical interest, are the sixteenth- and seventeenth-century small-scale county maps produced by Christopher Saxton, John Speed and their imitators, which were reissued in various forms down to the middle of the eighteenth century when they were finally superseded by the first one-inch surveys. Apart from providing evidence of the existence or not of a few features, in particular parks, the only practical value of the best series of this sort, those published by John Speed in 1610, lies in the inclusion of a bird's-eye view of the county town in the corner of each map. If redrawn with caution onto a modern base (e.g. a 1:500 Ordnance Survey plan of the 1870s) Speed's plans can be a useful starting point for a reconstruction of both the medieval topography of the town in question and of changes in the early modern period.

A more important seventeenth-century source, also issued in facsimile some years ago, is the remarkable atlas of road maps published by John Ogilby in 1675, which marks the beginning of both one inch to the mile mapping in England and also the convention of showing routes as strip-maps, a technique still used for road atlases today. Individual sheets from Ogilby's *Britannia*, or one of its many later derivatives, are frequently to be seen framed, glazed and coloured in print shops. This has tended to lead local historians to dismiss the maps as decorative rather than useful, the province of the map collector rather than the topographer, which is a mistake. Not only does the atlas as a whole provide a marvellous picture of the main road system of England and Wales fifty years before it began to be altered by the turnpike trusts, but each sheet contains a great deal of local information. Although only trunk routes are mapped in full, numerous minor roads are shown branching from main roads, as are dozens of bridges in each county, with a note as to whether they were wooden or stone-built. The layout of towns and villages is given in some detail, as is the nature of the country (inclosed, open field, woodland or parkland) through which each road passes. Not only can a considerable amount of local detail be extracted from an Ogilby road map, for a period for which little else may be available, but it is also possible to reconstruct the route on the ground today. This will identify later deviations built by turnpike trusts and may locate stretches of medieval and early modern main road that were never turnpiked or adopted by the county councils, often surviving as byways which give a convincing impression of what a medieval main road looked like.

Tithe maps

Whereas in towns the work of the Ordnance Survey may carry the history of large-scale mapping back to about 1850, in rural areas the next stage back from the second edition of the OS will normally be either the tithe map of the 1840s or, in areas subject to parliamentary inclosure of common fields (where tithes were commuted then, rather than under the Tithe Act), the inclosure map, usually dating from the second half of the eighteenth century or the first quarter of the nineteenth. Both are among the local historian's most basic tools.

Tithe, a render of one-tenth of the produce of land to the local church, was payable in England from early medieval times, as village churches were established by private landholders. Normally, the builder of such a church would assign to the parson the tithes of the land over which he was lord (i.e. his manor). The parson was responsible for the cure of souls in the area from which he received tithe (i.e. his parish). Thus arose the correspondence in many parts of the country between manor and parish boundaries. The coincidence was not universal: in some parishes estates were divided and there might be two or more manors with land in the parish; in other cases a manor might extend over all or part of more than one parish. But in large parts of midland and southern England parish boundaries, before they began to be changed by the building of new churches or the statutory reform of local government in the nineteenth century, represent not only the boundaries of very old ecclesiastical units, dating from the building of the village church in the eleventh or twelfth century, but possibly even older estate boundaries, perhaps of the tenth century. In northern England township boundaries are of similar antiquity, while in Wales so much less is known of early territorial organisation or the building of medieval churches that it is more difficult to determine the age of parish or hamlet boundaries. In all parts of the country, however, the boundaries shown on tithe maps are important historical documents in their own right, and a good clue to early estate boundaries as well as those of the local church. Inexplicable deviations by a boundary from what would seem to be its 'natural' course along a stream or the side of a wood may have an early medieval explanation, while the survival of detached 'islands' of one parish within the land of another (swept away by statute in the late nineteenth century) may reflect a Domesday or even older division of a vill between two estates.

Although originally tithe income was assigned to the parson of the church, in many parishes the 'advowson' of the living (the right to appoint the priest, which normally belonged to the man who built the church) was granted in the twelfth or thirteenth centuries to a religious house, either local or further afield, and with the advowson went the tithes. The abbey or monastery to which the tithes were thus appropriated would appoint a 'vicar' (from the Latin for 'deputy') to serve the church; they were remunerated by a share of the tithe income from the parish, typically about a third of the total (the 'small tithes'), while everything else (the 'great tithes') went to the 'rector' (i.e. ruler) of the church, meaning not an individual but a religious house. Hence arose the distinction between two different kinds of beneficed incumbent, since in a parish where the living was not appropriated the parson himself was the rector.

This distinction was maintained after the Dissolution, when tithes and advowsons owned by monasteries were sold by the Crown along with their temporal property. In many cases, a local landowner acquired the tithes of his parish and possibly also the advowson, so that the parson still received only a small income while local farmers, who may well have been the tenants of the tithe-owner, found themselves paying tithe to the same family rather than the parson. The difference between vicars and rectors in the modern church is purely titular (and has been further blurred by the creation of team ministries with 'team rectors' and 'team vicars') but until salaries replaced tithe as their main source of income the contrast in wealth and social standing could be considerable.

The early nineteenth-century campaign for tithe reform was concerned less with the position of the clergy than with the arbitrary and haphazard incidence of tithe. Traditionally payable in kind, tithe was normally rendered in cash in this period, but the amount was settled largely by a combination of local custom and will-power: an energetic impropriator or rector would extract more from reluctant tithe-payers than an absentee landowner or parson who relied on an agent for collection. More seriously, the purchaser of a farm or estate would not know for certain his liability to tithe on the land he acquired. To regularise the situation, and partly to meet the demands of opponents of tithe in any form, or those who viewed the accumulated wealth of the established church with hostility, Parliament in 1836 passed a Tithe Commutation Act. This provided for the conversion of tithe, in every parish where a similar arrangement had not already been made at the time of inclosure, from a payment in cash or kind to a 'rent-charge' on land, the amount varying according to the way in which the land was cultivated and the price of corn. A rent-charge is termed by lawyers an 'incorporeal hereditament', a piece of real property that exists but cannot be seen. Whoever received the tithes—rector, vicar, perpetual curate or lay impropriator—would henceforth receive a rent-charge, divided in many parishes between vicar and impropriator in the same proportions as before.

Following the model of the Poor Law Amendment Act (p. 146) the Act of 1836 set up a Tithe Commission in London: this dispatched assistant commissioners around the country to implement the Act, which affected about two-thirds of England and virtually all Wales. In each parish an assistant commissioner established the local facts by holding public meetings, commissioned a survey and drew up a provisional agreement between the tithe owners as to the rent-charge payable to each, according to previous practice and the new legislation. This agreement was then confirmed by the commissioners. The process obviously took some time and most awards under the 1836 Act date from the 1840s, with a few from before 1840 or after 1850.

The best known product of this process is the award drawn up by the assistant commissioners. After it had been confirmed, the original document formed part of the records of the Tithe Commission, which are now at the Public Record Office (p. 133). Two official copies were made, and sometimes further private copies, which may occasionally be printed, whereas the official texts were handwritten on printed forms. One copy was kept in the parish to which the award related and a second was sent to the diocesan bishop. These copies are for most purposes as reliable as the one held by the Tithe Commission, although strictly speaking only those bearing the commission's seal (as opposed to the signature of a commissioner) were accepted as first class copies.

The award consisted of two parts, a written agreement commuting the tithes of the parish, establishing the total rent-charge payable in lieu and dividing it between the tithe owners, and a schedule, setting out how much of the total rent-charge was payable on each parcel of land in the parish that was subject to tithe. Not all land was titheable: the built-up core of medieval towns was often tithe free, as was land owned in the Middle Ages by certain religious houses. Sometimes land not subject to tithe was scheduled separately, together with the reason for exemption, usually given as 'prescription', which amounted to an admission that tithe had never been paid on this land and its present owners had no intention of abandoning this privilege.

The need to list every parcel of land in the parish, at least outside a medieval borough, is what gives a tithe award its incomparable value to the topographer. Since there were no large-scale OS plans in 1836, surveys had to be commissioned specially for each tithe award, on a scale large enough to show every parcel, with each one numbered and keyed to the schedule. The scale chosen was usually between 12 and 25 inches to the mile. The maps had only to mark the boundaries of each parcel and are less detailed than OS plans, with few place-names and most buildings merely blocked-in. Canals are generally shown in full but early railways may appear merely as long thin parcels of land, with no attempt to mark the actual track. On the other hand, tithe maps recorded early medieval parish boundaries and islands of tithe-free former monastic land, as well as a host of modern features, which had been lost by the 1870s when the large-scale Ordnance Survey maps first appeared. Above all, they had a full written schedule accompanying them, describing the land in far more detail than an OS fieldbook (whose survival is in any case patchy).

The schedules attached to tithe awards were not compiled in such detail for the benefit of historians, nor to provide a local register of landowners and occupiers, although awards were often used in this way. Each column in the schedule had some practical administrative purpose in the 1840s and together they provide the fullest picture of the local landscape that one can normally obtain from anywhere, especially in a parish with poor estate records. First of all, the numbers on the map were used to identify parcels in the schedules, with a written description alongside. The latter may be a field-name, making tithe awards an invaluable source for modem names which can also be found in deeds and possibly related to much earlier forms of the same name, or it may be a term such as 'Homestead' (i.e. farmhouse), 'Barn, Stables, Yard &c', 'Ironworks, Furnaces, Foundry, Kilns &c', 'Mill, Leat, Mill Holme &c'; or it may just be the world 'Field' written dozens of times, with no names and just a gap where one might have hoped for a precise description of industrial premises. Not all awards are as full as others.

A discovery which frequently disappoints the new user of tithe awards is that the parcel numbers are not arranged numerically in the schedule. If you are seeking the owner and occupier of a particular field or building it is not normally possible to turn quickly from the map to the appropriate place in the award; you have to search through the book until you spot the number in one of the middle columns. The schedule is in fact arranged in alphabetical order of owner, with each tenant listed in the same order under his landlord's name. Institutional owners such as the parish, turnpike trust or chapel trustees generally come at the end. As with land tax assessments (p. 67), the terms 'owner' and 'occupier' can be accepted at face value by the beginner, but are open to some qualification. The former can include long leaseholders and also the trustees of an estate subject to a marriage settlement or of an owner who was under age. Occupiers are not always given in full, especially for cottages, where 'John Smith and others' occupying '12 Cottages, Premises &c' should if possible be checked with the census enumerator's book to find the names of the other 23 householders.

Other columns in the award give the acreage and state of cultivation of each parcel (occasionally actual crops are named), necessary since the Act laid down a different level of rent-charge for arable, meadow and pasture, and the amount payable to the tithe-owner or owners, the latter probably the information least used by local historians. There is finally a 'Remarks' column, used sometimes to note subsequent changes in ownership, the disappearance of a field under a railway line or, at least in the Tithe Commission copy, the redemption of the rent-charge by the landowner for a lump sum payment. In 1930 provision was made for the ultimate redemption of all remaining tithe rent-charge, a process that is now complete.

If you are simply looking at a tithe map to trace the existence or absence of a particular feature, such as your own house, plus its owner or occupier in 1840, then a visit to inspect the most accessible copy of the award will usually be sufficient. Apart from the complete set of central government copies at the PRO there should be a diocesan copy at the local record office (the National Library in Wales), and the parish copy should also have been deposited there, either by the church or the parish council, although this is the copy most likely to have disappeared.

If you are interested in exploring the history of your parish in depth, especially its landscape history, it is undoubtedly worth getting a complete copy of the tithe award—map and schedule—since it probably offers more scope for further research, backwards from the 1840s into the pre-industrial age, forwards to later OS maps, and sideways to the census enumerators' books, than any other source. Many long winter

evenings can happily be devoted to exploring all the facets of the tithe
map for your community, which you are unlikely to have time to
appreciate fully on a visit to the record office. Unfortunately, neither
the map nor the schedule is easy to copy cheaply with the resources
available in most record offices. Even where the map and schedule,
which were originally sewn together to form a single document, have
been separated, as is done in most offices, both remain too large to
copy on a conventional A3 photocopier. Because it is a bound volume,
the schedule cannot be copied on a large format plan-printer and the
map is often too fragile to be copied in this way. As usual, there is the
expensive option of photography, either at the local record office or the
PRO, or the unsatisfactory expedient of tracing the map. Another
possibility, where it is possible to obtain a photocopy of the first edition
of the six-inch Ordnance Survey map, is to transcribe details from the
map to this copy. In most country areas there will not be much change
between the 1840s and 1870s and you will then have a convenient
digest of the older map which can be related directly to later editions of
the as. For built-up areas the first edition of the 25-inch map may be a
better base to use. In either case, it will then be possible to make
further copies of the marked-up map at a plan-printing shop on which
to add information from the schedule.

Another solution to the problem of copying tithe awards is for a
record office to transfer all the material on to microfilm or microfiche,
from which A4 (or larger) prints can be made cheaply in most offices.
This facility is readily available for the whole of Wales at the National
Library; local historians in England will need to check with individual
record offices to see if any or all of their awards have been microfilmed. Where this has been done the map has usually been copied in at
least four sections (often many more in upland areas), and the prints
have to be joined together to recreate the entire map. Once this has been
done, it is best to make further copies from this master on single sheets
using a plan-printer, to save having to join up small sections every time
you want a new map. In the case of the schedule, although the originals
were prepared on forms somewhat larger than A3, the text should remain
legible as a series of A4 microprints, which are easier to file.

For a detailed study of a parish it is well worth transcribing the tithe
schedule in full, since so much information can be obtained from it,
especially in conjunction with the map. With a manual project, it is best
to use a separate sheet for each occupier's holding, possibly using a

form which reproduces the columns of the original schedule. These can then be sorted by occupier, as opposed to owner, and the occupiers traced in other contemporary records, notably the census enumerators' books. This operation also brings together all the land rented by the same person from different owners, so that one can establish a tenant farmer's total acreage in the parish. Alternatively, it is possible to make an index with a card for every parcel, which can also be sorted by parcel number, field name (with the possibility of adding cross-references to the cards from deeds or estate surveys which mention the same name), or by land usage. This involves far more work, particularly for a large parish, and writing the names of the major owners a great many times. It is, of course, a task for which a simple database running on a home computer is ideally suited, since one can then print all the information from the schedule arranged in a variety of ways and add data from other sources.

Some of the uses to which you can put a tithe award have already been touched on. Essentially, they provide a virtually complete picture of a community from which to develop work in different directions. To begin with, it will probably be worth marking up different copies of the plan with field-names, the names of owners, the names of occupiers, and land usage. The latter can be compared with conditions today, a pleasant and not usually over-strenuous field exercise in a country parish, or in some parts of the country with a Land Utilization map of the 1940s. The value of using tithe map field names to identify premises conveyed in stray deeds has already been mentioned (p. 66). Some mid nineteenth-century deeds also use tithe map parcel numbers, although this practice was superseded when the 25-inch OS became available. The same applies to rentals, terriers and other estate material surviving among landowners' muniments. Here the tithe map is especially useful, when there are no estate maps, in giving a topographical dimension to estate acquisitions and disposals recorded only in deeds. Using the summarised details of ownership and occupation at the end of the schedule, one can work out the division of landownership in the parish in the 1840s (Family A had 70 per cent of the land, Family B had 10 per cent, and so on), or the average size of farms, including variations between mixed farms and those with no arable, or those on the main estate and any owner-occupied freeholds.

The tithe map is useful for much more besides the history of farming and landownership. Industrial premises may be mapped on a large scale here and nowhere else, and details of ownership and occupation given, useful in tracing documentary material where no business records survive (p. 76). If you are interested in the history of your house, or of every house in the village, the tithe map is almost always the best place to start, largely because of the ownership and tenancy information it supplies. If your house (which typically will have no deeds more than fifty years old, even if the building itself is clearly much older) proves to have been part of a local estate in 1840 that again may be a key to locating deeds, leases or other documents (p. 62). Since most farmhouse and cottage building was entirely traditional up to 1840, the tithe map is a good place to begin a survey of local vernacular architecture (p. 125). Note each building marked on the tithe map on a more recent map and see how many survive, either at all or relatively unaltered. See how many of the farms of 1840 are still working agricultural holdings, perhaps looking also at old six-inch maps to see when farmhouses were abandoned as such.

Most of these suggestions relate to a rural community but tithe maps are also invaluable for the suburban topographer. Many towns show little suburban sprawl by 1840; certainly what are now the outer London suburbs were simply villages at this date. Here the pattern of landownership as revealed by the tithe map is often the key to what happened in the 1890s or 1930s. Try transcribing the estate boundaries of 1840 on to a 25-inch map post-dating the main period of suburban growth. You may find that the network of avenues, closes and drives fits into the pattern of landownership two generations earlier, or that parts of the parish, inexplicably developed much earlier or much later than their neighbours, belonged to one particular owner in 1840. From here you may be able to trace a sale catalogue of 1920 advertising the estate as desirable building land, or the first deed belonging to your 1936 semi may be a conveyance from a descendant of the owner in the tithe award to Wimpey or New Ideal Homes. For earlier suburbs, it may become clear that by the 1880s the mansion had been let, the family were living in South Kensington and so land was shaved off the edge of the old deer park to make way for Beech Villas or Laburnum Lodge, for which the oldest deed is a ninety-nine-year building lease reserving a ground rent to the departed landowner.

For older built-up areas the tithe award can be disappointing. The core of medieval boroughs was often tithe-free and the map will simply outline the area and give it a single parcel number described in the schedule as 'Town of Barchester'. For some towns, however, there are very detailed tithe awards, in which the schedule lists the contents of each plot ('House, Overgateway, Workshop, Dye-House, Boiler-House, Steam Engine, Wash-House, Bakery, Croft and Premises' is quite possible), which, with the information about ownership and occupation, are an invaluable starting-point for any exploration of earlier or later history. Infilling of medieval burgage plots behind the main street frontage, thus creating slum 'courts' and 'yards', can be traced by comparing the tithe map (on which there may be very little infill) with a large-scale plan of the 1870s (on which there may be a great deal, perhaps christened 'Pleasant View' or 'Robinson's Row' after the owner on the tithe map). The function of many nineteenth-century factory buildings can be identified from an urban tithe award, which may also be the key to locating on the ground property conveyed in miscellaneous deeds in solicitors' collections, if one of them supplies the name of an owner or occupier in the 1840s.

The other major use to which both urban and rural tithe awards can be put is for what some years ago tended to be dignified with the name 'house repopulation': trying to identify on the tithe map all the householders who appear in one of the census enumerators' books now available (1841-91). Most commonly one uses 1841 or 1851, usually the latter, even if the tithe award is nearer in date to 1841, since the second census conducted by the Registrar General was more carefully compiled and the replies are somewhat more detailed. Census enumerators' books have been described (pp. 35-9), as have tithe awards, and in theory it is simple to find the same occupier in both and locate his house on the map and then on the ground, especially as census enumerations normally had an underlying topographical basis. In practice, it is often rather difficult, and few who have tried this with a place of any size have managed to locate every household in the census on the tithe map. Sometimes an enumerator did not copy schedules into his book systematically, or did not give sufficiently detailed addresses in built-up areas. There may have been too much change between 1840 and 1851, so that whole streets in the census do not appear on the map. This is where the deficiencies of the tithe award's list of occupiers become obvious. Head leaseholders may appear in the award, whereas the census will list a dozen undertenants renting all or part of the house. 'Several' is not unknown as a name in the 'Occupier' column of a schedule. The easiest community in which to tackle house repopulation is an upland parish in which settlement was dispersed, all the farms were individually named in both the tithe award and the census, and, if most of them were freeholders, there is little change over a ten-year period. In a tightly packed nucleated village, where 'Glebe Cottage', 'The Old Chantry', 'Maltings' and similar names date from *c.* 1970 and there are no house names in the census, it is much more difficult, as it is in small towns, which is where there is most likely to be a surfeit of census over tithe households.

These comments should not discourage local investigators from trying house repopulation in their own community, since it makes a satisfying change from the *Daily Telegraph* crossword and residents of Glebe Cottage today are invariably entertained to know who lived there in 1851. It may even induce them to let you see their deeds, which will allow you to work out a full history of their house. What is needed, apart from complete copies of both the census and tithe award and a good deal of time and patience, is local knowledge, full use of other material, especially directories and electoral registers (pp. 29, 74), and a few stable landmarks to begin with, such as pubs on street corners, which will be clearly identifiable in several sources. A complete project of this kind makes it possible to give a geographical dimension to all the questions one can ask of census material (pp. 35-9) and fleshes out what is known of the occupiers of farms in the 1840s from the tithe map alone. House repopulation and other work on the tithe map and census can also make an attractive and fairly simple publication for an individual or group wishing to interest people in the recent past, since so many surviving houses will be described in a booklet or 'trail' summarising the results of the project.

Inclosure awards

The tithe award may be the earliest map of your parish as a whole, and possibly the only one before the 1870s. The local historian working on a community where tithe was commuted before 1836 may find, however, that the absence of a tithe award is compensated for by the existence of a detailed inclosure award of a somewhat earlier date.

After about 1750 a local Act of Parliament became the most common device for effecting, usually on a larger scale than previously, a process that had gone on in all communities since time immemorial, the 'inclosure' of land. Inclosure does not begin with the parliamentary inclosure movement of this period; on the contrary, this marks its final phase, ending in growing opposition to further destruction of common land. Whether achieved by local Act, general Act, agreement enrolled in one of the central courts, or simply private agreement, inclosure describes one of two operations affecting land usage in a community. It might mean enlarging the area of land within a parish that was 'culti-vated' in the widest sense (it may only have become permanent pasture after inclosure, not arable or meadow), by dividing the common land between the freeholders of the manor; or it might mean the rearrange-ment of existing arable land (and usually also meadow) so that each farmer henceforth cultivated his own land himself, rather than took part in a communal system based on large open fields in which the farmers had dispersed strips of land.

On a medieval manor all the tenants, free and unfree, had customary rights over what was legally known as 'waste'. This might be barren moorland which supported some summer grazing, or a village green in the heart of the settlement used for recreation and the gathering of fuel as well as grazing animals, or an area of common on the edge of the village of perhaps 50 or 100 acres. Between about 1750 and 1850, and especially during the period 1780-1820, millions of acres of such 'waste', the greater part of it moorland and mountain rather than village green, were inclosed under local Acts and the land divided between the owners of the existing inclosed land of the parish, the successors of the medieval free tenants of the manor. Acts of this kind were passed for parishes in every county in England and Wales, but particularly affected upland counties where more uninclosed moorland had survived earlier land clearance.

In those parts of England where in the Middle Ages arable land was cultivated, in whole or in part, in a two- or three-field system of communal farming, with fields divided into unfenced strips, and where these fields had not already been swept away, a similar phase of parliamentary inclosure during the same period virtually completed the process of inclosing common field arable. Instead of extending the cultivated area, inclosure Acts provided for the division of open fields into closes, and the allocation of the land to the freeholders in propor-tion to their previous holding in the fields. This rearrangement of property rights was best enshrined, according to eighteenth-century opinion, in an Act of Parliament, and most of the remaining open field of midland and eastern England disappeared in this way. In the north and west and in Wales the much smaller proportion of arable cultivated in common in the Middle Ages had mostly been inclosed much earlier by private agreement, so that very few inclosure Acts for these regions are concerned with open fields.

When a common field parish was inclosed by Act, the opportunity was usually taken to allot a share of the land involved to the rector (or other tithe owner) in lieu of tithes, thus extinguishing the payment of tithe by the other landowners. For this reason such parishes normally lack an award drawn up under the 1836 Tithe Act, or else the award deals only with a small portion of the parish and there is no comprehensive map and schedule as described in the previous section. On the other hand, the inclosure of waste was not generally combined with the commutation of tithe and so parishes subject to Acts of this sort will usually also have tithe maps.

Both types of inclosure affected the pattern of landownership as well as land use, although how far parliamentary inclosure led to the disappearance of the small landowner is now less clear than was once believed. But there was a tendency for large estates to grow larger and small freeholders to disappear as such, as local historians may discover in their own parish by comparing estate surveys of different dates or looking at land tax assessments.

The inclosure of both open fields and common waste often led to the building of new farms in a parish, which may have left a fairly obvious architectural legacy today in the form of a group of buildings all clearly dating from the early nineteenth century. In open field regions these new farmsteads will generally be out in the former fields and replaced the older farmhouses on the village street, which often declined into labourers' cottages. Where moorland was inclosed, new farms would be established on the former waste beyond the limits of medieval clearance, cultivating (or at least grazing) newly inclosed marginal land. In parishes where there was no parliamentary inclosure, or any other documentary evidence of inclosure, it is sometimes possible to trace the topographical results of early private inclosure by looking carefully at the tithe map for farms built 'out in the fields', away from older settlement. They often have names including the element 'Field', mostly obviously 'Old Field Farm', meaning a medieval open field, not a close. For parishes subject to parliamentary inclosure, it should be possible to trace the same process by comparing the inclosure map with later maps.

After 1792 an inclosure award executed by commissioners named in a local Act had to be enrolled among the records of quarter sessions, so that it should now be in the county record office, although copies also survive in estate and parish records. In some counties the clerk of the peace collected awards before 1792. How extensive and thus how useful it will be for local landscape history depends on how thorough-going was the inclosure. Where a medieval three-field system had survived wholly or largely intact, as thousands did in the Midland Plain, Lincolnshire and East Anglia, an award may include a map of the entire parish, illustrating the existing layout, with that proposed by the commissioners after inclosure superimposed on an open-field plan. Where only remnants of an open-field system survived from earlier inclosure the plan may show merely the area to be inclosed. The same is true of awards affecting only a village green, a small common, or strips of waste alongside the highway, which will be mapped as a series of sketches with sufficient adjoining land shown to identify the parcels affected. If several thousand acres were being inclosed on the edge of the parish, there may be an outline map of a more or less featureless moor, divided up into neat square blocks for the new owners to take up. In every case, the plan will be accompanied by a written schedule listing the owners and the land allotted to them, with each parcel numbered on both the plan and schedule.

Where an inclosure award and a tithe map are both available it is obviously worth comparing the two. By transcribing details from the inclosure map on to a copy of the tithe map you may be able to make a substantial leap backwards towards a picture of the medieval landscape, removing half a dozen post-1780 farms or a thousand acres of suspiciously square fields on the edge of the moor which form no part of the medieval farming history of the community. Where there is no tithe award the next available map will often be the large-scale Ordnance Survey of the 1870s, which again forms a convenient base on which to add details from the inclosure award.

It is also worth pursuing the details of inclosure on the ground. As well as following up new farmsteads, one can look at new housing or industry which may have appeared on inclosed waste that was of little agricultural value, or check that the process of inclosure actually took place as the commissioners intended. Some awards were not imple-mented for several years, and occasionally the economic margin to which it was worth inclosing land receded faster than the new owner could build fences, so that some waste was in fact never inclosed as an award said it should have been.

As well as dividing and allotting land, inclosure commissioners normally took the opportunity to straighten existing highways across land being inclosed, or create new roads, although they could not alter the arrangements on land already inclosed. The term 'highways' includes footpaths and bridlepaths, and since, inclosure awards deposited with the clerk of the peace are public records which have always been in official custody, the evidence they supply as to the existence and status of rights of way is admissible in law. It is for this reason that archivists are sometimes pursued by property owners or ramblers seeking to deny or establish the existence of a right of way, or by pony club enthusiasts hoping to have footpaths restored to bridlepath status. More broadly, awards are a useful source for the history of roads and tracks in a community (see also pp. 79-80), since inclosure often led to substantial changes in their layout.

Deposited plans

Quarter sessions records contain another class of plans, those which from 1792 had to be deposited with the clerk of the peace (and with Parliament) in advance of an application for a local Act authorising the building of a canal or (from various later dates) a turnpike road, railway, dock or other types of public works. A copy of the plan had to be supplied to the clerk of every county through which the canal, railway or whatever would pass and it is worth stressing that plans were deposited for hundreds of schemes which were never proceeded with, especially during the 'Railway Manias' of the mid nineteenth century.

Early canal and turnpike plans are usually on too small a scale to be of much value, but the railway plans are much more detailed. All are useful for transport history (pp. 80-1) but local historians not interested in railways sometimes fail to appreciate their general value. The idea of having a plan publicly available was to allow landowners affected by the scheme to see exactly where the route of the railway fell and whose land would be taken. The plans are thus strip-maps, marking the line and at least a hundred yards of country on either side, with the parcels numbered and scheduled in a 'book of reference', which supplies the usual details (acreage, owner, occupier, usage) for a tract of country where a railway was built or proposed. In towns, where existing property might have to be demolished, the plan will often be drawn on a larger scale and cover a wider area. For towns not otherwise well served by early plans it is worth checking those deposited for proposed railways to see if any has an inset providing an enlarged plan of part or all of the town, which will probably be superior to the tithe map and possibly a generation earlier than the first edition of the 25-inch map. Unfortunately it is very time-consuming to list deposited plans comprehensively so as to include every parish covered. Early schemes and those that were actually executed usually stand out, but in some offices many plans simply appear in a catalogue as 'Midland Railway. 1876. Additional Lines &c.', which leaves a lot to the imagination.

Estate maps

Inclosure awards and deposited plans may be indexed separately in a record office, or they may be included in a general index of maps and plans, the rest of which will be found mainly in deposited collections. Most of the maps in the latter category will be estate surveys, touched on in the section on landownership (p. 61), which are invaluable, when used with other material such as rentals and deeds, for recreating the past landscape and the history of farming.

Medieval landholders did not commission maps of their property—to them a 'survey' meant a written description—but from the end of the sixteenth century to the middle of the nineteenth owners employed surveyors to produce maps of their property, usually accompanied by a 'terrier' listing tenants and holdings. Since about 1880 large land-owners, public and private, have mostly relied on marking up 25-inch or larger OS maps to identify their property. As with estate records generally, it is unwise to be over-optimistic in searching for surviving maps. Surveys were expensive and are more likely to have been made for large estates than small ones. They were not frequently redone: surveys that have been heavily used in estate offices, and more especially their terriers, will often contain half a century or more of annotation and updating. Above all, they were not plans commissioned by munificent landowners who wished to provide the community with a beautifully coloured large-scale plan of their village; they are plans of what one person owned. Where this was most of the land in a parish, the map will amount to a parish map; in other cases it may consist simply of small sketches locating isolated parcels in parishes in which most of the land belonged to others. Since landownership tended to be heavily divided in old towns, estate maps are usually least informative for such places, whereas for some rural parishes, from as early as 1600, there are some magnificent examples in local record offices and important holdings at the Public Record Office. The latter are catalogued in a published volume and are obviously strongest for towns with a service connection or estates owned by the Duchy of Lancaster or another adjunct of the crown.

However comprehensive or sketchy their coverage of a particular place, estate maps provide similar information for all the parishes included in a survey. The parcels shown on the plans are numbered or lettered and a schedule in one corner of the map, on facing pages of a volume, or in a separate book supplies the name of the tenant, the name, acreage and state of cultivation (arable, meadow, pasture etc.) of each parcel, possibly the terms on which the land was held (at will, copyhold, leasehold etc.), and sometimes comments about the holding. Where a landowner was planning changes, or acquired an estate that appeared to have been neglected, the surveyor was often asked to report, either separately or in the terrier, on possible improvements in buildings, tenants, tenures or land usage, comments which can often be very illuminating.

On a large estate there may be two or more surveys at different dates; more typically there will be one eighteenth- or early nineteenth-century map, either a single sheet or part of an atlas. Many, with extensive use of colour and elaborate cartouches and scales, are objects of great beauty. Few are suitable for photocopying, but such is their usefulness that it is worth transcribing the detail on to a copy of an early six-inch Ordnance Survey map or even having a map pro-fessionally photographed. An eighteenth-century estate survey may be a better source of field-names than the tithe map; it may portray a landscape that by 1840 had been much altered by industry; or it may show a landscape about to be changed by inclosure or emparking. Comparison between an estate map and the tithe map may reveal the disappearance of individual houses or even a whole village, or the earlier map may show a moated site that had become 'Mote Croft' by 1840, with indeterminate earthworks surviving on the ground.

Seventeenth- or eighteenth-century estate maps often show houses as bird's-eye (or axonometric) sketches, apparently in realistic detail. In a village where much farmhouse and cottage architecture has survived from the period of the Great Rebuilding (c. 1540-1700) it may be possible to compare such drawings with standing structures to judge whether they can be relied upon for those buildings that have disappeared. Attempts to link the evidence of sketches to the number of hearths in tax assessments (p. 143) are perhaps less convincing.

Using maps

Most local historians have some interest in the history of the landscape and for such an investigation maps are obviously essential. The best way of proceeding is probably to start with a sequence of Ordnance Survey six-inch maps to see how the picture has changed over the last century, then look at all the evidence for landownership, farming and land usage which the tithe map (or, in its absence, the inclosure award) can provide. If there is any earlier map material for the parish this can often best be transcribed on to a tithe map or six-inch base, so that it can be related directly to firm nineteenth-century evidence. Working in this way you will then be able to produce a series of maps from the present back to 1840 (or earlier using an inclosure award), and then with luck 'peel away' relatively modern features from the tithe map towards a speculative but reasoned view of the landscape in medieval times. An inclosure map redrawn to tithe map scale will enable you to remove post-inclosure closes and farmsteads; a deposited plan will show what the area was like before a canal was built; either may locate pre-turnpike or pre-inclosure roads.

To carry the history of the landscape further back will involve the use of other, more specialised evidence: the clues supplied by minor place-names for the former existence of open fields where these were not mapped before inclosure; archaeological evidence for deserted, shrunken or moved settlements; former tracks not marked on any map; medieval industrial sites indicated only by slight earthworks. Material of this kind is discussed in the next chapter and by combining fieldwork with the careful study of maps it should be possible for any community, urban or rural, to produce at least an outline sketch-plan of the parish in medieval times. In a publication, either standing alone in a booklet on landscape history or as part of a chapter on the Middle Ages in a larger parish study, a map of this kind, with a commentary on how it was compiled, is likely to be of much greater interest than an reiteration of unconnected references to the place from printed medieval public records, which is what so much old-fashioned writing on local communities in the this period consists of.

Local historians interested in maps are generally well served by finding-aids, because the material is in such demand in libraries and record offices. There is usually at least a card index to the holdings of a particular repository and for several counties a handlist or a full-scale bibliography has been published. At an early stage in almost any research project, therefore, local historians should check what map sources there are for their area. As with manuscripts, it is probably best to work backwards from relatively straightforward material—older editions of the large-scale Ordnance Survey maps—and then try to relate the evidence of earlier privately produced maps to the first six-inch or 25-inch map of the area. Taken in isolation, a scrappy eight-eenth-century estate plan or a small-scale deposited plan for an early canal may seem impossible to relate to the present-day topography of the same area. When examined as the last, rather than the first, stage in a step-by-step exploration of the landscape, however, it will fit in more easily and may supply clues as to the appearance of the same stretch of country three centuries earlier.

Not only are maps, especially major sources like the tithe map, invaluable for the general history of a community, but they add an extra dimension to almost any kind of enquiry. It is surprising, for example, how few family historians seem to use maps to give a sense of place to their research and to see what a village looked like when their ancestors were enumerated there. Even fewer think of looking at tithe awards, which name dozens, sometimes hundreds of heads of household. Similarly with those interested in a particular house or an industrial building: if all else fails, it will always be on the Ordnance Survey map and probably on a tithe map, in which case you will have the names of owner and occupier on which to hang further enquiries. Maps are all-important for local history and they are also great fun!

Landscapes and Buildings

Trends and structures

The last chapter set out the main map sources available to local historians and suggested some ways in which evidence of this kind could be used to trace either individual features or the development of the landscape as a whole. It is now conventional wisdom to emphasise that maps and documents are only half the story and that for a complete picture one must also look at the landscape itself and buildings therein. This fascination with visual evidence on the part of English antiquaries is not new; what has changed, gradually since the beginning of the twentieth century and much more rapidly in the last forty or fifty years, is the way in which the study of physical evidence has erected itself into a separate discipline, which has in turn split into a number of different fields of varying academic value. To try to bring them all back together again it became popular a few years ago to argue for 'total archaeology' or, if you were an historian, 'total history', terms which would have seemed strange to an eighteenth- or nineteenth-century antiquary, for whom there was no dichotomy between 'monuments and muniments' and who was equally at home with either. At local level, in field clubs or among the curators of museums, there is still no real division, but on a grander scale several fields of study have emerged, allegedly with their own techniques and invariably with their own journals.

The first change was the extension of archaeological research beyond the limits achieved by Haverfield and his contemporaries before the First World War, through which the archaeology of Roman Britain became an acceptable companion for prehistoric archaeology. The development of Romano-British archaeology alongside the study of prehistory up to the turn of the century is well illustrated by the articles on these topics in early volumes of VCH, whereas those on the archaeology of Anglo-Saxon and medieval England show a less sure use of field evidence. Between the two World Wars the value of archaeology for the study of the period between 500 and 1100 became established;

after 1945 the same discipline extended its scope to the sixteenth century, leading to the establishment of the journal *Medieval Archaeology* in 1957. A smaller group subsequently promoted 'post-medieval archaeology', urging the use of field evidence of all kinds as an adjunct to sixteenth-, seventeenth- and eighteenth-century history, and in 1967 the first issue of *Post-Medieval Archaeology* duly appeared.

Meanwhile a changing view of society led to new interests in architectural history, which in the nineteenth century established itself as a scholarly study less by the attention paid to documents (a discipline only adopted with some reluctance by many practitioners within the last half-century) than by the development of the measured drawing as a means of recording standing structures. To a small extent from the turn of the century, but much more so after 1945, architectural historians became interested not only in churches, manor houses and public buildings, but in the homes of the mass of the people, the farmhouses and cottages which survived in most parts of Britain from the sixteenth century or later. Thus was 'vernacular architecture' born, concerned with buildings made of local materials by local craftsmen uninfluenced by conventions of 'polite' design. Its main field of study has remained the period from the sixteenth century, when the bulk of the population for the first time lived in houses intended to last more than one generation, to the nineteenth, when the coming of the railway meant that building materials could be distributed nationally and the design of working-class housing ceased to vary greatly between different regions. Before the sixteenth century peasant houses have normally to be investigated archaeologically. The close links between those interested in standing structures and those who have come to this period from an interest in excavation have led to a hybrid approach which owes as much to archaeology as to architectural recording. A similar technique has been applied to medieval churches, where these are available for thorough study: the standing structure is stripped archaeologically and excavations may be conducted both inside and outside the walls of the present building.

Many of those involved in medieval and post-medieval archaeology and the study of vernacular architecture have also been concerned with the promotion of 'landscape history'. Here the emphasis is on the 'total landscape', on trying to reconstruct what a particular stretch of country looked like a hundred, five hundred, a thousand or three thousand years ago. Again, this is not really a new pursuit, but over the last thirty years has attracted sufficient support to establish another national society and a new journal, *Landscape Studies*, first published in 1970. As its practitioners argue, landscape history involves the application of several disciplines to the same, usually fairly limited, area. The material of landscape history includes the results of archaeological excavation or the recording of earthworks or other field monuments; the surveying of polite or vernacular buildings or other structures; the analysis of field- and place-names; the use of maps and topographical documents; and, if really tackled in depth, the use of material from several scientific disciplines, especially geology and botany. Like most of the activities described in this chapter, landscape history 'done properly' requires a range of skills not usually combined in one person and, if conducted over an area of any size, considerable resources. On the other hand— unlike, for example, archaeological excavation—it is also something the individual amateur can do on a more modest scale with useful results.

In the first edition of this book, I reiterated the severely critical views I had then held for at least ten years concerning the contribution—or rather lack of any worthwhile contribution—which the variety of activities embraced since the early 1960s under the name of 'industrial archaeology' had made to the study of the Industrial Revolution. As I argued then, much of what had been done during this period had been misdirected and largely wasted effort, except to secure the preservation of some of the more important physical monuments of the Industrial Revolution which would otherwise have been lost. On the other hand, a great deal *was* demolished in these years without any proper record being made, largely because of a reluctance of those interested in industrial archaeology to master the basic disciplines of archaeological and architectural recording. Those responsible for establishing the Society for Medieval Archaeology or its post-medieval counterpart generally came from one of two backgrounds. Either they were experienced in excavating earlier archaeological sites and applied these skills to later remains, or they were trained in recording standing structures, whether they were earthworks or buildings. In either case, one produces measured drawings, or at least field sketches, and photo- graphs, irrespective of whether the remains have first to be excavated. This procedure, developed since archaeology became a separate discipline in the nineteenth century, rarely appealed to the first generation of industrial archaeologists. Much was said and written about methodology without its being realised that there were really no 'techniques of industrial archaeology'. All that was wanted were drawings and photographs. Work such as that done by the medieval and post-medieval archaeologists, or the vernacular architects, might usefully have been applied to many post-1750 sites which have now been swept away, but the opportunity was lost.

Since the early 1980s there have been some signs that industrial archaeology is maturing and may yet evolve into a worthwhile field of study. It cannot be said that the Association for Industrial Archaeology or its journal, *AIA Review*, has contributed much to this raising of standards: rather it has been the work of the three Ancient Monuments Commissions in England, Scotland and Wales (or, to be more precise, the efforts of a limited number of individuals on the staffs of those bodies), all of whom have demonstrated how industrial monuments should be investigated, recorded and published, drawing on the skills developed by these bodies since their establishment at the beginning of the twentieth century. While the English and Welsh commissions have both produced several excellent monographs on particular topics or places, the Scottish Commission has gone one stage further and published a fine general survey comparable to the two well known syntheses of work on vernacular housing issued some years earlier by the other commissions.

The nearest equivalent for England is a recent volume by Michael Stratton and Barrie Trinder on *Industrial England*, which demonstrates how the careful analytical study of factories and other buildings can yield useful historical evidence of value to economic historians, most of whom have treated the claims of industrial archaeology with well merited scepticism. This book, which has grown out of the work of both authors at the Ironbridge Institute, the other organisation which has done most to create something worthwhile out of interest in the physical evidence of industrialisation, deserves to have considerable influence on how the study of industrial monuments (or at least industrial buildings, since the authors do not deal in as much detail with other types of field evidence) develops over the next decade or two.

The value of field evidence

The overall impact of this multifaceted growth of interest in archaeology, buildings and the landscape is that few local historians now need reminding of the importance of field evidence. Arguably, most amateur enthusiasts never did. Although in recent years many people's interest in local history has developed from first pursuing the origins of their own family, for others the fascination still begins when they find something—an old building, an unexplained earthwork, or just a hole in the ground—and want to know what it is or was. They assume their local library or record office will be able to tell them and usually end up by being shown, possibly for the first time, large-scale Ordnance Survey maps spanning the last hundred years (p. 86).

If those who begin in this way are told of other map sources and where to find them, their enthusiasm may develop into a full study of their local landscape. The alternative starting-point, which should lead to the same end-result, is for someone to be shown an old map and to see something they did not know about, such as water-mill, or a colliery tramway, or some odd-looking unidentified feature. It is a natural reaction to ask, 'I wonder if there's anything left of that' and to go and look at the spot on the ground. A generation ago that could have led to the discovery of an abandoned water-mill with its wheel and perhaps some machinery left inside, or the stone sleeper-blocks of an early nineteenth-century horse-operated railway. Today, after a period in which both the urban and rural landscape have changed very rapidly and much evidence of past life has been removed for ever, there is less scope for discoveries of this kind (the mill will have been swept away or it will have become a private house or a heritage centre; the tramroad will have been destroyed by opencasting, land reclamation or road-widening), but any work on landscape history must include an appreciation of the importance of both written and non-written evidence and of how each relates to the other.

This latter point applies with especial force to industrial archaeology. One of the many silly aspects of this pursuit in its early years was the misdirected energy spent investigating on the ground what was already known from Ordnance Survey maps. Thus people drove hundreds of miles taking indifferent pictures of derelict collieries. This contributed as much to our knowledge of the coal industry as half an hour spent photocopying old OS maps, i.e. establishing the existence and location of nineteenth-century collieries. Had the time been spent measuring headstocks or other surface structures (or even taking record photographs to something approaching Royal Commission standards) the work might have been of some value, but it rarely reached that stage. Since the publication of the second edition of the Ordnance Survey (p. 86), the British landscape has been recorded in great detail on contemporary maps. By all means go and visit these places to see how they have changed, or look at buildings of the period or landscapes that have survived relatively unaltered. This is to use the landscape for illustration, a perfectly legitimate pursuit and one which has served to enhance many people's interest in the past, or encourage an interest that had previously been absent or latent. It is not, on the other hand, making use of the landscape as evidence, as one tries to do for earlier periods for which there are no maps. Similarly, if you find some feature on the ground which you wish to identify, start by looking at the map sources for the area. If whatever it is proves to be the product of the last century or so, it may well be possible to find out what it was simply from a sequence of large-scale maps and establish that it is not as old as you thought, or as other people told you.

This sort of common sense, still denied by some of the more blinkered proponents of the claims of industrial archaeology (and denied to a much greater extent in the past), can be rationalised thus. For any period of British history since the Roman invasion the historian has two main sources of evidence: that which is written, mostly on parchment or paper (to a small extent on stone or other materials), and that which survives either on or beneath the ground. Whereas for periods prior to the Roman invasion, history must be written almost entirely from archaeological evidence (which sometimes leads to the mistaken idea that 'archaeology' is the study of early history, instead of a method of enquiry used by historians and prehistorians), from the first century onwards archaeology is one of several techniques used by historians (or, in practice, archaeological discoveries are so used, since the actual discovery is usually done by archaeologists). The development of archaeology during the twentieth century, and parallel changes in the study of architectural history, have led to the use of physical evidence down to a much later period than was considered worthwhile a hundred years ago, because it has been realised that in some circumstances this evidence can supply information not available from documents.

The extent to which historians draw on archaeological evidence diminishes as one approaches the present day, since documents become available and supply information more easily and completely than archaeological evidence can. Thus we would know little about the way of life of the ruling class of Roman Britain had substantial remains of their homes not survived to be discovered, excavated and in some cases preserved over the last two centuries. In the case of their medieval counterparts, we know something of the houses they lived in from surviving documents, including some illustrations, but our knowledge would again be much poorer had a number of castles not survived in reasonably complete condition and been investigated. Even in the early modern period, for which records survive in greater quantity, it is still useful to be able to examine those great houses of the sixteenth and seventeenth centuries which still stand to determine how they were built and used. On the other hand, if all the remaining Victorian great houses were to disappear tomorrow, a valuable part of our national heritage would have been lost, but the study of nineteenth-century social history or building technology would not have suffered irreparably, since both subjects are studied principally from written (often by this date, printed) sources.

Down to what date archaeological evidence retains more than illustrative value will vary. Thus, had archaeologists not uncovered and interpreted the remains of a large timber-framed hall belonging to the early medieval rulers of Northumbria at Yeavering, we would know little about the social and economic organisation of that kingdom in the age of Beowulf, since few of its administrative or judicial records survive. By contrast, the surviving remains of Tutbury Castle in Staffordshire are visually much more impressive, but they do not contribute anything substantial to our knowledge of how the Duchy of Lancaster was administered, even though Tutbury was one of the centres of that administration. Instead, we look at the voluminous records of the duchy. On the other hand, the remains of this and other castles are an important source for the study of medieval military architecture, an illustration of the point that field evidence may be of greater value down to a later date for certain kinds of history than for others. Buildings and field monuments probably add little to the study of political history beyond the end of the Anglo-Saxon period, whereas similar structures remain important for the history of technology (and some aspects of more general economic history) until at least the eighteenth century and possibly, in some circumstances, the nineteenth. It is probably impossible to set a definite cut-off date, although the dictum enunciated at its foundation thirty years ago by the Society for Post-Medieval Archaeology that the value of archaeological evidence diminishes sharply with the onset of industrialisation (as far more information becomes available from both published sources and archives) and for this reason the period covered by their journal would in general extend from around 1500 to about 1750 has stood the test of time.

This point illustrates one of the difficulties which supporters of industrial archaeology have had in convincing both archaeologists and historians that what they are doing is really worthwhile. The other problem is connected with the simple truth that archaeological evidence is only of value when it has been made available in a usable form. The same is true in a somewhat different way of much historical research (imagine studying the history of medieval central government without the published calendars or unpublished finding-aids available at the PRO) but whereas documents can be gathered into record offices and kept there safely until there is time to explore them, this is often not possible in the case of physical evidence. Excavation is a non-repeatable exercise and unless the results of the enquiry are published the information is lost for ever. Similarly, if an important building is not systematically recorded before demolition that evidence will also be lost. Probably the main reason why industrial archaeology has contributed little to mainstream historical studies is because of the general superiority of written over physical evidence in the period of the Industrial Revolution. The other reason is the dismal failure until recently of those interested in physical evidence to make their material available in the same way as those studying earlier remains have done. In some cases, this shortcoming is being rectified, for example through the work of the English Royal Commission on early textile mills in the Midlands. In others, of which the iron industry, with its important legacy of surviving blast furnace remains of the period 1650-1850, is still as good an example as it was when I made the point in the first edition of this book, there has been much less progress. Only for a handful of these sites are there measured drawings available in print, and no-one has yet attempted to use the evidence they supply to discuss the evolution of either the blast furnace itself or the layout of ironworks as a whole in this period.

The local historian interested in industrial history should perhaps bear two points in mind. In general, most of the evidence will come from maps and documents and, while it may be interesting to go out and look at old buildings, they will probably not add much to what is known about a particular industry. Secondly, in circumstances where physical evidence can supply some of the answers (and the example of the iron industry is certainly a case in point) the evidence must be investigated with the same thoroughness as that for earlier periods, and must be studied in close conjunction with conventional historical sources. The same is true of earlier periods in which the starting point of some investigation may be field evidence: it is essential to integrate the study of written evidence, especially maps, with what is found on the ground.

Local history on the ground

The previous chapters have said something about written sources and maps; what about the practical use of field evidence in local history? Sometimes, this will simply mean the use of published or unpublished findings of previous investigators, especially with sites accessible only by excavation, as the conduct of this type of archaeological research on a large scale is extremely expensive and highly skilled. Since the 1970s, full time archaeological 'units', which in their day have been *ad hoc* committees funded by grants from central and local government, sections of local authority planning departments maintained directly from public funds, and independent trusts relying as much on contracts from developers as money from local authorities, have been responsible for most excavation (as well as field surveys) carried out in advance of redevelopment. This is what became known twenty years ago as 'rescue' archaeology, although the work is now more securely integrated into the planning process and confrontations between archaeologists and bulldozers are in general a thing of the past. At the same time, some museums and university archaeology departments have continued to conduct 'research' excavations and surveys on sites which are not directly threatened with destruction, and there remains scope in some parts of the country for amateur volunteers to take part in small-scale excavations under skilled direction. On the other hand, it remains the case, as introductory textbooks on archaeology have long emphasised, that unskilled amateurs should not interfere with areas of archaeological interest, whether statutorily protected or not. Local historians interested in the evolution of the landscape should be aware of evidence derived from excavation, but through using the results of other people's research, not digging holes in the ground themselves.

Some of the sources of archaeological information have already been mentioned. The most important will probably the annual journal of the county antiquarian society (p. 13), which remains the outlet for most excavation reports. This is obviously worth checking for any work on sites in your area, while the library may have offprints of articles from the national journals describing investigations of more than local interest. Conversely, you may know of (or even have taken part in) excavations whose results have not been published anywhere, in which case it may be worth pursuing notebooks, drawings or photographs in the hands of a local museum, library or record office, or contacting the excavator or his family to see if any records survive.

Even if no excavations appear to have taken place in your parish, it is unlikely that there will have been no archaeological discoveries of any kind. Although excavation is the type of research that attracts most attention, there is a long tradition of fieldwork above ground in British archaeology, which is vastly cheaper to undertake and is the aspect of the subject which has fused with other types of field enquiry to become landscape history. This is the area in which the individual amateur can make the largest contribution, but before starting enquiries of one's own, it is as well to see what has already been discovered. Again, the main source of published information will be the county journal, other local publications and, old fashioned though they may seem, the archaeological chapters of VCH (pp. 15, 111). These will usually have been written before the First World War, but at least provide a sound resumé of the state of knowledge at that time, collecting together and analysing references to discoveries from the seventeenth century onwards.

Since the summaries in VCH were published, many more sites have of course been discovered but only in a limited number of cases has later work been brought together in county-wide (or thematic) gazetteers, while minor finds often remain unpublished. Traditionally, both local museums and county archaeological societies maintained card indexes of archaeological discoveries in their area, based on published references and other finds brought to their attention. These have now been subsumed in more elaborate 'sites and monuments records' compiled by local archaeological units, in which the information may still be stored manually or it may be automated. Irrespective of the format or the degree of sophistication with which the database can be interrogated, the essential feature of all such systems is that they locate discoveries as precisely as possible on the ground, using the National Grid. If therefore you are interested in the landscape history of your parish, it is worth asking to see all the entries in the SMR for your area as a starting point for your own investigations. It is also, of course, worth sending in details of any discoveries you yourself make to enhance the record for your area.

Among the sources used to compile the SMRs maintained by local units is the relevant portion of the index of archaeological features compiled for the entire country by the former archaeology branch of the Ordnance Survey, which was used for the 'period maps' compiled by the OS, such as that for Roman Britain, and the publication of 'antiquities' on modern OS maps of all scale, although far more features were included in the index than were ever published. The work of maintaining a national archive of archaeological information (in the widest sense of the phrase) has passed in recent years in England to the National Monuments Record, which forms part of the work of the Royal Commission on Ancient and Historical Monuments. There has been a parallel transfer of material relating to Wales to the separate NMR maintained by the Welsh Royal Commission. The three commissions (there is another serving Scotland) were set up in 1907 with the object of compiling inventories of monuments (including buildings dating from before 1714 as well as archaeological features) and publishing the results as a series of gazetteers for each county.

The progress of this vast undertaking, particularly in England, was always slow and has now been abandoned, although a few volumes will continue to appear for counties where a traditional inventory has been underway for some years. Instead, the staff of the commissions undertake field recording and store the results of their discoveries initially in the three National Monuments Records, alongside informa-tion derived from a variety of other sources, including notes supplied by members of the public and the staff of local archaeological units. Some of the data thus accumulated is used for a variety of publications by the three commissions, which these days deal with particular types of monument, either in the country as a whole or in a particular region, rather than all the features discovered in a given area. The other major change in recent years has been an extension of the chronological scope of the commissions' work to include recent buildings and other features; indeed, as I have suggested earlier in this chapter, much of the best recording and publication of industrial monuments over the last ten years has been done by the staff of all three commissions.

The National Monuments Record was established during the Second World War as the National Buildings Record, an archive of photographs and drawings of important structures threatened with destruction by enemy action. Although the scope of both the English and Welsh NMRs is now much wider, they retain very large collections of photographs of buildings, which are constantly growing as the work of the photographic staff of the two Royal Commissions continues. Anyone interested in recording buildings in their area (in my view a particularly worthwhile activity for a local photographic society looking for a group project to tackle) would do well to study the advice given in a handbook written by one of the English commission's photographers, or simply look at the published work of the staff of all three bodies, which represents modern architectural record photography at its best. All three commissions also collect air photographs, of which there are a number of other public and private collections.

The two Royal Commissions for England and Wales are happy to answer postal enquiries asking for details of what is available in their respective NMRs about a particular site and can supply copies of photographs, drawings and record cards. It is also possible for members of the public to visit both offices to locate material themselves. The English Commission is at Kemble Drive, Swindon SN2 6GZ; the Welsh Commission's address is Plas Crug, Aberystwyth SY23 2HP.

In the 1970s there was a revival of interest in compiling maps of past landscapes, on much more ambitious lines (and on a larger scale) than those accompanying the archaeological chapters of VCH or the Ordnance Survey period maps. During the vogue for 'total archaeology' in these years (and the initial enthusiasm for landscape history around the time the Society for Landscape Studies was established) it was felt that if all the available evidence could be brought together it would be possible to produce far more detailed maps of a particular area than had ever been done before; in a few cases, notably a survey of the West Riding, impressive results were achieved. Fashions in landscape history seem to have moved on in recent years, but this should not deter local historians interested in their own parish from thinking along these lines. At the very least, it should be possible to draw together archaeological discoveries, either your own or other people's, into a series of simple 'period maps'. For the prehistoric and Roman periods this will usually involve marking such discoveries on a base map showing only the natural features in the modern landscape. Although from time to time exponents of the idea of 'continuity' in the landscape have made ambitious claims for the extent to which Roman or even prehistoric features (e.g. territorial boundaries or fields) are embedded in much later landscapes, it is generally impossible to substantiate ideas of this kind. On the other hand, as the last chapter suggested (pp. 109-10), the practised local historian should be able to recognise clues on large-scale nineteenth-century maps which suggest what the medieval landscape looked like, and to 'peel away' later features, working backwards towards Domesday Book.

How much an actual inspection of the landscape can contribute to post-Roman landscape history depends largely on what has happened to it in the much more recent past. The landscape may have been the most valuable historical document which Maitland's generation possessed, but he was writing at the end of the nineteenth century, before a revolution in the farming industry, a great extension of the built-up area, the building of a modern motorway system, and large-scale opencast coalworking and quarrying. Some more recent writers, notably W.G. Hoskins and his followers, have also spoken in extravagant terms of the need to get mud on boots and the exhilaration of striding across a landscape barely changed since the days of Chaucer.

To local historians in some parts of the country this advice will have a hollow ring. Dating hedgerows by counting the number of species is hardly possible if most of the hedgerows in your parish have disappeared in the last thirty years, or the fields themselves have been completely changed by gravel extraction. Many minor earthworks marked but not identified on the OS 25-inch maps of the 1880s have now gone for ever and their history can only be sought from documents and other maps. The same may well be true in your parish of one of the best known of all rural landscape features, the corrugated 'ridge and furrow' effect given to some open field arable in the Middle Ages. Some very good examples of ridge and furrow survive in the Midlands and elsewhere and are regularly photographed for books and television programmes extolling the delights of history on the ground. Much more has been ploughed out, either recently by modern deep ploughing, or over a longer period if the open fields disappeared in the sixteenth or seventeenth centuries and the land remained arable. Even in areas of later parliamentary inclosure, it is often easier to map the open fields by careful redrawing of old maps or air photographs on to modern base material than by surveying field evidence. Similarly, it is still possible to find ditches and banks on the ground which once marked the boundaries of medieval parks or even Anglo-Saxon estates, but there are many areas where evidence of this kind has all been swept away and can only be recovered by looking closely at field boundaries and field-names recorded on the tithe map. At the other end of the spectrum, the scope for fieldwork on industrial sites is far less today than was the case thirty years ago, thanks to the extensive programme of land reclamation in former coal mining areas and the clearance and redevelopment of the industrial areas of the great conurbations.

History on the ground will always be fun, and in most parts of the country it is still possible to make worthwhile discoveries, simply by looking more closely than anyone has previously at a particular stretch of country. On the other hand, there are some areas (including, as it happens, the two in which I grew up and have spent most of my working life) where the scope for fieldwork is more limited, and maps and documents are likely to be a more fruitful source than the present-day landscape. This is also the case with those bits of the landscape whose owners or tenants have yet to be convinced of the attractions of history on the ground and prefer not to have people tramping across their farm, scrapyard or wherever.

It was the Ordnance Survey map, rather than the landscape itself, that was once described as a marvellous palimpsest that we still do not fully understand. The OS maps of the late nineteenth century are still there to study; the landscape they portrayed, with all its clues to a much earlier period, has since been swept away in many areas. In a sense, of course, this bears out the claim that the landscape is an important historical resource, but not in quite the way that statement is usually meant. If much of your parish is now covered with modern housing estates, or if most of the land has been affected by opencast coal-working or land reclamation, or if the site of the huge engineering works which overshadowed all the streets in your part of the town is now a retail park, then it remains true that the present-day landscape reflects the history of the area. Unfortunately, the changes of recent decades have been so sweeping that the resulting landscape may contain only evidence of what has happened in the last twenty, thirty or forty years, whereas in 1900 it might have been possible to look at features dating from every century since Anglo-Saxon times.

Buildings in the landscape

Until the end of the nineteenth century, and in many cases until a much later date, local antiquaries took account of only two buildings in a parish, the Anglican church and the manor house. Even the great house, as opposed to its occupiers, only began to receive attention towards the end of the Victorian period. One of the most important aspects of the revolution in local studies since 1945 has been the growth of interest in more modest domestic buildings and, more recently, Nonconformist chapels and meeting houses. A few students of 'folklife' or traditional building materials were already looking at local architectural styles before the First World War, but over the last forty years an almost entirely new field of study, vernacular architecture, has developed, with its own national organisation, journal and monograph literature. At the same time, the Ancient Monuments Commissions, English Heritage, Cadw and the National Trust have all taken far greater interest in small domestic buildings. Parallel with this, there has been a continuing interest in more traditional aspects of architectural history, taking in the surviving secular buildings of the Middle Ages and the country houses of the sixteenth century and later. New areas have developed here also, notably an interest in landscape parks and gardens around great (or not so great) houses, or a new enthusiasm for Victorian, Edwardian and Thirties buildings, rural and urban. Nineteenth-century working class housing and later council estates have also attracted attention.

These changes have affected the study of local communities in various ways, apart from the quite different but equally important shift in our view of what should be preserved from the past. Perhaps above all, buildings, polite as well as vernacular, are now seen as 'documents' supplying important historical evidence and not merely as illustrations of a bygone age. Like all source material, they will only yield useful information if studied intelligently. In the case of vernacular buildings, both urban and rural, a systematic procedure was evolved for their study in the 1950s at the school of architecture at Manchester University, which was simplified for wider consumption in R.W. Brunskill's *Illustrated Handbook of Vernacular Architecture*. The system involved isolating the component parts of a small or medium-sized domestic building (roof, walls, doors, chimney stacks and so on); the style or position of these features within the building (e.g. hipped roof, lateral chimney stack, central doorway); and the materials of which each component is built (this includes distinguishing, for example, different brickwork bonds or methods of stonemasonry). Finally, the position of the building in relation to others, especially farm buildings, and its general alignment are noted. Although ticking boxes on record cards is no longer widely favoured as a means of recording field evidence of any kind, this approach had a number of attractions. It was comprehensive and well worked out; it could be applied to any part of the country and to both rural and urban building. The information required could normally be obtained from an external inspection and collected quickly without a measured survey. Above all, by asking detailed questions about every aspect of a building, it forced the observer to look closely at its salient features.

The Manchester system of recording vernacular buildings was intended to provide a rapid but reasonably detailed summary record of local styles and materials across fairly large regions (ultimately, it was hoped, the whole country) that could be followed up by a more detailed examination of typical or particularly interesting buildings. A few regional studies of this kind were completed at Manchester in the 1950s and later, combining widespread summary examination of the domestic architecture of a district with measured drawings of selected buildings. This work was concentrated mainly in rural areas but during the same period the Leicester local history department became the home of several urban studies, which tend to present problems not susceptible to summary analysis because of the greater complexity of change in towns. Here the approach was a very full, virtually house-by-house survey, involving large numbers of measured drawings and a close study of documents. Unfortunately, because work of this kind is so detailed, publication tended to lag a long way behind the initial fieldwork. By contrast, for rural housing, two general studies, one on England and the other on Wales, written by staff of the respective Royal Commissions, were published in the 1970s, drawing on examples recorded by the commissions throughout the country. There have also been a few further regional surveys since those undertaken at Manchester many years ago, as well as numerous more specialised contributions to *Vernacular Architecture* and the archaeological journals.

For the local historian interested in old buildings there is thus a large general literature on what has already been discovered and how such buildings should be studied. In most parts of England there remains much scope for the amateur fieldworker, although in Wales, where the Royal Commission has less ground to cover and (at least in the past) the Museum of Welsh Life (the former Welsh Folk Museum) has also been active, there may be less. In some areas, a simple summary survey would still be useful; elsewhere, the basic features of the vernacular tradition are now fairly well established, although more detailed surveys, with measured drawings of particular houses, may not have been done. Closer examination of buildings from the inside as well as the outside may also reveal a more complicated history than was apparent during a summary survey. This is almost always the case in towns, where there is also more chance of supplementing field evidence with that of documents, such as deeds, rentals or other estate records (pp. 59-67), or probate inventories (pp. 70-2). Apart from inventories, this material is less plentiful for cottages and farmhouses in the countryside.

For every county in England there is a volume in the 'Buildings of England' series founded by Sir Nikolaus Pevsner, and the parallel series in Wales is now making more rapid progress than was the case for some years. These gazetteers do not normally contain detailed descriptions of many vernacular buildings but are useful for churches and the larger domestic buildings, and also for their lengthy introductions on the building history of a county in general. Probably more useful for the local historian working on a particular parish will be the unpublished but accessible 'Lists of Buildings of Special Architectural or Historic Interest', describing buildings 'listed' by the Secretary of State for the Environment (on the advice of English Heritage) or the Welsh Secretary (advised by Cadw) as being worthy of protection. The lists also include features protected under different legislation as 'ancient monuments' (which these days need not be of any great age, but must be of national significance). Local libraries or planning departments will have copies of the lists for their areas, which are usually short enough for a particular parish to have photocopied at reasonable expense. They are a good starting point for a local survey, although even the more recent lists (and much more those compiled when the system was first set up under the 1947 Planning Act) are based on a fairly brief examination of the buildings concerned, with limited use of maps or other historical evidence, and a local investigator should be able to amplify the descriptions considerably. It is, of course, open to any member of the public, or a local group, to write to English Heritage or Cadw proposing a building (or other structure) for listing or, alternatively, scheduling as an ancient monument.

Some readers interested in old buildings may simply wish to establish the date of their own home. For them, sources mentioned in this chapter and in that on maps, as well as the relevant section of Chapter 3 (pp. 59-69) should provide a fairly full guide; because of the popularity of 'tracing the history of your house' there are now several books which cover this topic in detail and some record offices have leaflets on the subject.

As with any specialised field, some of those interested in vernacular architecture seem to regard the study of old buildings as an end in itself and show little interest in the evidence the buildings provide even for the history of technology, much less for general social and economic history. On a broader level, however, a model was devised some years ago to account for the survival of the corpus of buildings that forms the raw material in this field. On the one hand, vernacular architecture is concerned with buildings made of locally available materials and built according to local rather than national (or 'polite') ideas of design. There is thus a 'vernacular threshold', which moves across time and progressively excludes a greater proportion of the total housing stock. Medieval great houses, including castles, were not 'vernacular', nor by the seventeenth and eighteenth centuries were many more modest town and country houses. In the second half of the nineteenth century, the distribution by rail of cheap mass-produced buildings materials, coupled with the introduction of uniform building regulations throughout the country after 1875, brought an end to the use of local materials and designs, first in towns and then in the countryside, so that by 1900 even the most modest working-class houses had ceased to be vernacular.

Another feature of the housing stock in the past which limits the material available for study is the permanency of the structure. Medieval great houses were built to last and many have done so to the present day; medieval peasant houses were not and do not normally survive, although there are some relatively modest medieval houses, both urban and rural, still standing. During the period characterised as the 'Great Rebuilding' (roughly 1540 to 1700 but varying between different regions) the majority of the population came to live, for the first time, in permanent houses, of which again large numbers have survived. Only in the eighteenth or even nineteenth century did the poorest inhabitants of the poorest regions of the north and west (including parts of Wales) live in such houses.

The overall effect of these two forces—the vernacular threshold and permanence of structure—means that the subject has tended to be concerned most with the early modern period, plus some larger houses which have survived from the Middle Ages and small cottages of a rather later period. It is not concerned with medieval great houses or with nineteenth-century 'bye-law' housing, neither of which were vernacular, nor with medieval peasant houses, remains of which have to be recovered by excavation.

Local historians seeking to use the evidence of vernacular architecture in a study of their community, rather than those who are merely interested in surveying old buildings, should be able to apply this model to what they see around them. The impermanence of medieval cottages and the general renewal of the housing stock in the sixteenth and seventeenth centuries are well established concepts, but it is also important to look for other upswings in the building cycle since the Great Rebuilding. In some areas there was little or no comprehensive rebuilding after 1700 until the 1950s or even later, so that in much of midland and southern England it was possible, until the extensive changes wrought to the rural housing stock over the last twenty or thirty years, to see largely unaltered evidence for the Great Rebuilding in every village. In other parts of the country, however, comparatively little survives from this period because of later changes. In particular, the extensive renewal of farmhouses and farm buildings that seems to have taken place in regions benefiting from the prosperous farming of the Napoleonic War years (1793-1815) may have swept away most or all older building. This is just as much a 'Great Rebuilding' as the better known one two hundred years earlier, and for most parts of the country can best be appreciated by looking at surviving farmhouses, since documentary evidence at local level is often limited, Alternatively, the farms and cottages in a village may all date from the late nineteenth century and may all have been built by a single owner, often in a distinctive, uniform and not necessarily vernacular style. This too may be historical evidence not preserved anywhere else, if the estate in question has no surviving muniments.

Endless study of different kinds of dovetails or chamfers may fascinate students of vernacular architecture, but for the material to be of wider value it must be seen in a broader context. Housing is a form of expenditure, one to which most people accord a high priority. If they are well off they will spend more money on better housing; if they are poor they will make their existing housing last longer. The date of most of the surviving houses in your village is therefore a guide to its changing prosperity since the appearance of permanent housing for the majority of the people in the sixteenth century or later.

To use this evidence you must first work out the date of the housing stock and then see how this evidence relates to that from other sources. If there is little sign of change between the Great Rebuilding and the coming of the M4 to within ten miles of the village then that is evidence for a lack of prosperity between about 1700 and 1970, of the village having been unaffected by parliamentary inclosure, the Industrial Revolution, the Napoleonic War, High Farming, the coming of the railways, or the Housing Acts of 1919 and later. Conversely, a lack of renewal in the late nineteenth century may reflect the effect of the agricultural depression between the 1870s and the turn of the century on the community. If, by contrast, your parish has virtually no building surviving from before 1800 and most of the farms are square Georgian boxes then the community may well have been transformed by inclosure and the prosperity of farming in lowland areas around the beginning of the nineteenth century. If half the cottages have changed little since the Great Rebuilding but the other half all seem to have been done up about 1900 and have the same person's initials on them, that may be evidence that one of the two estates concerned employed a minor Arts and Crafts movement architect to restore the property. Changes of this kind may be traceable only from visual evidence; alternatively, such evidence may lead to a search for documents which confirm or refute an idea. If, for example, your parish contains a secondary settlement made up of what were originally rather poor early nineteenth-century cottages it is worth looking at maps to see whether they were built on a piece of common waste by people unable to get housing in the main village. If all the villages in your area have a neat row of post-1945 (or older) council houses near their edge read through the minutes of the rural district council (p. 56-7) to see why the authority decided to build them.

Urban housing should be looked at in the same way, although with older structures there may be considerable technical problems of interpretation if the building has been extensively and repeatedly altered.

The basic idea is the same, however: the age-profile of the housing stock of a community is an index of its wealth over time, combined with the impact of public or private individuals or corporations, or the supply of land for building or the supply of buildings themselves. Thus, if your town was greatly enlarged (or even built from scratch) around the end of the twelfth century it was because (a) that was a period of rapid economic growth, and (b) the lord of the manor decided to develop his estate by enlarging or building a town. If your town centre was completely rebuilt in the 1960s or 1970s then the first of those explanations still applies, except that for 'lord of the manor' one substitutes 'property developer' or 'local authority'.

Less dramatic change to individual buildings or streets can be explained in the same way. At its simplest, one can date streets added to the town in the nineteenth century, by looking either at the housing on them or at maps and documents. On streets that have been built up since the Middle Ages there will typically be a mixture of property, perhaps including a house that actually incorporates some late medieval fabric, but it is the age of the bulk of the property that is important in using physical evidence for more general local history. The present appearance of High Street, Burford, should not just be drooled over, as thousands of tourists do every summer during a brief visit, but seen partly as a reflection of the late medieval and early modern wealth of this important centre of the Cotswold wool trade; and equally as a consequence of (a) the relative decline of the town in the period 1700-1900, from which there is little building, and (b) the wealth of the town and rigour of development control since 1945, which together account for the careful conservation of High Street today. The survival of so many relatively early buildings also reflects modern views of what one does with sixteenth- and seventeenth-century houses: had Burford become the home of some major Victorian industry most of that housing would have been demolished as old-fashioned and insanitary.

Local historians often belong to conservation or amenity societies and, when such activities were more popular than they are now, did much to campaign against the destruction of old buildings. They should not, however, succumb to the temptation to see an attractive street frontage merely as evidence that their community is 'old', 'historic' or 'unspoiled'. A particularly irritating development in recent years has been the appearance of the epithet 'Historic Market Town' on brown road signs encouraging motorists to to stop and spend money in country towns (such as Burford) which happen to have retained a number of buildings dating from before about 1750. Few such places can claim to have been the scene of 'historic' events in the way in which, say, Manchester or Birmingham can; they may well have had markets of some local importance in the Middle Ages but so, for example, did Chesterfield, Barnsley and Rotherham, none of which is perceived by the average tourist as being 'historic', since all have been subject to extensive rebuilding since the Industrial Revolution. Equally, it is quite wrong to say that places such as the last three 'have no history' or that towns like Uxbridge or Slough 'have been ruined' by redevelopment over the last fifty years. Everywhere has a history and often that history is most obviously illustrated by the buildings one can see today.

Buildings, whether considered singly, in streets or in whole communities, are evidence, just like documents and the landscape. They are of course useful evidence for students of building technology but they may also supply information about the past economy of a community which is obtainable from no other source—or they may at least illustrate aspects of economic or political history which are studied principally from written sources. Local historians should look past the next base-cruck and try to work out why a family had the money to put a new double wind-braced through-purlin roof on its house.

CHAPTER SIX

The Public Record Office and other National Collections

Since this book is aimed at beginners, it may seem wrong to include a chapter concerned largely with a repository which is undoubtedly not the place to start local history research and which is not used at all by many amateurs. On the other hand, all local historians come across references to the Public Record Office and most are interested in knowing what it is and what its holdings consist of, not least because the older textbooks, especially Cox's *How to Write the History of a Parish*, dwell heavily on centrally preserved sources, which also feature extensively in the footnotes to parish histories in the Victoria County History. One reason, of course, why most local historians make limited use of the PRO is that the average amateur enthusiast living in the provinces, especially with a regular job outside education, only occasionally has the chance to visit London during the working day. Even those living within easy reach of the office may well have to fit trips to the PRO into annual leave, so for this reason alone it is worth giving some advice to help make visits as effective as possible. This chapter also mentions some of the other national libraries and record repositories used by local historians. In general, full addresses, phone numbers etc. have not been included, since these are prone to change and are available in the various guides to record offices listed under Further Reading (p. 180).

The Public Record Office: a guide for new readers

As explained earlier (pp. 13-14), the PRO was established in 1838 to provide a single home for the judicial and administrative records of central government which had previously been kept in the Tower of London and elsewhere, mostly in unsatisfactory conditions. Into it were gathered the records of the two great institutions of medieval administration, the Chancery and the Exchequer, the records of the central judiciary, and those of several minor courts. As the nineteenth-century revolution in government progressed, so the volume of records increased and more recent material was transferred to the PRO from an increasing number of departments. In the 1850s the office acquired purpose-built premises in Chancery Lane, which were to remain its main home until the first phase of the new buildings at Kew was opened in 1977. In 1996 Chancery Lane was closed and the entire office moved to Ruskin Avenue, Kew, where a second phase of building now makes it possible to concentrate almost all staff and holdings on a single site for the first time for seventy years.

For a long period prior to the move to Kew, the PRO had been facing acute problems of lack of space for both readers and documents. Although there has been a tendency on the part of some users to decry the abandonment of the historic buildings in Chancery Lane, this criticism ignores both the impossibility of finding a large enough site for a new office in central London and the inconvenience of the old building, especially over the last twenty or thirty years. Those who complain about the tedious journey on the Underground or the South Circular Road needed to reach Kew tend to forget the shabby and frequently overcrowded search-rooms at Chancery Lane, the lack of any catering facilities apart from a temperamental drinks machine, the variable cleanliness of the lavatories, the poor working conditions for the repository staff (which did nothing for morale), the irritation of finding that the document you wanted to see was stored at Hayes and would take a week to reach Chancery Lane, or simply the unexplained delay in the production of items that were supposed to be on the premises. There is something distinctly depressing, as well as quintessentially English, about the way in which there has been far more public criticism of the closure of Chancery Lane than pride in the completion at Kew of probably the world's finest national record repository, able to provide for the first time in over a century an appropriate home for what is undoubtedly the world's most important archive of government records.

If the holdings of a county record office can seem overwhelming on a first visit, then the contents of the PRO, covering as they do almost every department of one of the most sophisticated, highly centralised governments in the world, are bound to be much more difficult to grasp. Even the vast range of publications relating to the contents of the PRO, ranging from complete transcripts of certain documents, through calendars of the main administrative records of medieval government, to simple lists of modern material, takes some time to get to know. Even more than with a local office, it is essential to read as much as possible about the PRO before you set foot in the building, so as to understand what you will find and how to make best use of your time there.

The best starting point is arguably still the three-volume *Guide to the Contents of the Public Record Office* published by HMSO in the 1960s, even though this has been superseded as a working manual by the 'Current Guide', which is available in word-processed loose-leaf format at the PRO itself, but is otherwise published (rather expensively) only on microfiche. The advantage of the old *Guide* is that, although out of print, it can be found in most reference libraries and does provide a good grounding in how the holdings of the office are organised. Equally, although many new classes of material have been transferred to the office since the book was published and others have been rearranged, the *Guide* is still useful as an introduction to the intricacies of medieval and early modern central administration, whose records have been subject to less change over the last thirty years. In addition, my own *Record Sources for Local History* (1987), although written in the period when the holdings were divided between Chancery Lane and Kew and slightly out-of-date in other respects, may still be useful in identifying material of particular interest to local historians.

The most fundamental point about the PRO is that it houses the records of central government (of England, Great Britain, the United Kingdom and the British Empire, depending on the period concerned) and the superior courts of law as they have accumulated in official custody since the eleventh century; unlike a local record office it does not (except in a few very special cases) collect material as gifts or deposits. A few departments retain their own historic records, rather than transfer them to the PRO; in addition, the records of the Scottish Office and its predecessors, the Scottish offices of some other departments, and the Scottish superior courts, are kept at the Scottish Record Office (recently renamed the National Archives of Scotland) in Edinburgh, while those of the government of Northern Ireland and the Northern Ireland Office are at the Public Record Office of Northern Ireland in Belfast. Some judicial records relating to Wales have, on separate occasions, been presented or transferred to the National Library of Wales (pp. 158-9).

All the records at the PRO are divided into 'groups', each of which is divided into one or more 'classes', while each class consists of a number (often a large number) of 'pieces', each of which has an individual reference. Understanding this threefold arrangement is a good start towards unravelling the complexities of the office. A 'group' at the PRO normally means the records of a particular court (Chancery, Exchequer, Common Pleas etc.) or department (Home Office, Foreign Office, Treasury etc). The subdivision into classes varies according to the nature of each department's work and is impossible to summarise here. Each group has what is known as a 'lettercode' which is applied to all the records belonging to that group. For many years after the introduction of these codes in 1923, the PRO used a simple system of initials (such as C for the records of the Chancery, E for Exchequer, HO for Home Office and so on) but this was abandoned some time ago for new groups in favour of an arbitrary two-letter system (AA, AB, AC ... ZZ). Thus the records of the War Office, some of which have been at the PRO since the nineteenth century, have the code WO, whereas those of the Welsh Office, which was only established in 1965, have references beginning BD.

Within each group, each type of record forms a separate class, with its own class number. Thus, to take a couple of examples used a good deal by local historians, ED 21 are files relating to elementary schools established after 1870, which form one class within the Ministry of Education group; E 179 are lay subsidy assessments and similar documents preserved among the very extensive records of the Exchequer. In passing, it is worth noting that when presented correctly in footnotes or elsewhere a PRO reference does not have full stops in or after the lettercode (since this is a mnemonic, not an abbreviation) and that there is a space (not an oblique stroke) between the lettercode and the class number. There is, on the other hand, a stroke between the class number and piece number (and again before any sub-number). Thus a full reference to a tax assessment in the class just mentioned would take the form E 179/256/17.

The old *Guide* describes every class that was in the PRO when the it was published but it does not list the pieces within each class whose numbers you need to order the documents to the search-room. For this you need a 'class list', which is where the jungle of the PRO finding-aids becomes more complex, although considerable efforts have been made to simplify matters since the whole of the office moved to Kew.

On the other hand, the situation remains more complicated for the local historian living some distance from London who wishes to make as much use as possible of published finding-aids before visiting the PRO.

Every class available for study at Kew has been listed but only a small proportion of these lists have been published, and those that have do not form a single series. For some classes, the *Guide* lists what published finding-aids there are (transcripts, calendars or descriptive lists) and these can normally be found in a large reference library or university library; they are catalogued in a free booklet that used to be issued by the old HM Stationery Office, which can also be found in most reference libraries. The oldest publications are those of the early nineteenth-century Record Commission, which are generally full transcripts of basic medieval sources, such as Henry VIII's survey of church wealth of 1535, *Valor Ecclesiasticus*, the book referred to on p. 28 as one whose title is often incomprehensibly abbreviated because it is so well known. In a slightly different category are the long series of calendars (bound in dark green cloth) published by the PRO since the late nineteenth century (although the series is now being wound up), providing detailed summaries in English of the main administrative records of the medieval Chancery, the sixteenth- and seventeenth-century State Paper Office and a few other departments. These form the *Cal.* family who also turn up, to the bafflement of beginners, in the footnotes to scholarly works (*Cal.Pat.R., Cal.Cl.R., Cal.S.P.Dom.* etc.) and are explained in the *Guide*. Thirdly, the PRO issued in the past a series of Lists & Indexes, supplying piece numbers for certain classes. These are the converse of the relevant section of the *Guide*: they say nothing about what the documents contain but give full reference numbers for ordering items in the search-room.

While the existence of calendars and lists is indicated in the *Guide*, nothing is said there (because the series had not been inaugurated) about a newer set of publications, those of the List & Index Society, which was established by PRO users to reproduce unpublished finding aids kept only on the search-room shelves, and to distribute them to subscribing libraries (and a few individuals). This series, which can be recognised from some distance by its unattractive green and yellow binding, simply prints whatever was available at the PRO for a particular class at the time the volume was published, usually a typed list with manuscript amendments. Because the series was set up by record users it has concentrated on heavily used classes where the lack of a published list was proving frustrating to searchers outside London, and many of these are of local interest. Like the older finding-aids, the series is available in university and larger public libraries.

As with a local record office, only more so, it is essential to go to the PRO with some idea of what you want to see, if possible with exact references to three documents (the most that will be produced at once) with which to get started. Often one can pick up an initial reference from a footnote in a printed book, although there is no point going to the PRO to check a medieval reference if you will not be able to read the document, or just to see whether the editors of the relevant volume of the *Calendar of Patent Rolls* have got all the details right (they almost certainly will, and in any case patent rolls are not easy to read). Similarly, although the PRO staff are very good at answering letters, there is no general index of personal and place-names at the office from which they can identify all the references to your village or family, and the staff can certainly not undertake genealogical searches for you. It is unproductive to turn up at the PRO just to see what they have got on your parish without having some idea where to look, or to arrive with the name of an ancestor hoping to find a series of references to him in some huge index.

It is obviously impossible in a book such as this to describe, or even list, all the classes in the PRO which contain material of local interest; I attempted to do something on these lines in *Record Sources*. Here, I have simply referred to a few categories of central government records which are fairly easy to read, have not been included in published calendars, and will yield information about local communities. This includes some genealogical material, although one of the PRO's own publications covers this ground more thoroughly. First, however, a word about actually getting into the place.

If you have a fairly clear idea of what you wish to see at the office, or at least know which classes you wish to search and have established that there are no published finding-aids for them, there is no need to write in advance of a visit. Alternatively, if you write to the office with a reasonably specific enquiry, the reply will probably identify some documents (or at least a class) worth searching and invite you either to make a visit or employ a record agent to do the work for you. The office may also send copies of any of its excellent free guides to particular categories of material that appear to be relevant to your enquiry, and possibly its list of record agents, as well as a general leaflet giving details of how to find the office, opening times, car-parking arrangements and so on. The office is just off the South Circular Road about a mile south of Kew Bridge, not far from the end of the M4. It is just over five minutes walk from Kew Gardens Underground station on the District Line and North London Line and slightly further from the Railtrack station at Kew Bridge. Access on foot is via Ruskin Avenue; access by car, leading to a car-park that is probably going to need enlarging in the not too distant future, is via the next turning off the South Circular as one drives east. Both are signed from the main road.

The opening hours of any record office are liable to change, but at the time of writing the PRO opens six days week (i.e. including Saturdays) from 9 a.m. to 5 p.m., with late opening on Tuesday and Thursday. The decision to open two evenings a week and on Saturdays is only one of a number of changes made by the office since its move to Kew intended to improve its service to the public.

At the main entrance, which is clearly signed from the car-park, your bags will be searched and new readers will be directed to another desk where you will be issued with a reader's ticket, for which you will need some means of identification but not a photograph. You then proceed into another ground floor area that contains a large cafeteria (where, unlike most such places, you can eat your own food, since there is nowhere else in the building to do so), a shop selling both the PRO's own publications and other useful titles, a cloakroom with lockers for bags, lavatories, and public telephones. After depositing coats, bags and as much other impedimenta as possible, you are free to go through the barrier (operated by the bar-code incorporated in your reader's ticket) and upstairs to the reference rooms and reading rooms.

The main reading room is on the first floor, to the left of the stairs; to get to it you walk through two smaller rooms in which the lists and other finding-aids are kept on open access. To the right of the stairs is a room in which documents read on microfilm or microfiche are kept, beyond which is the very fine PRO library (now open to readers as well as staff). On the second floor the public area used to be known as the Map Room and is still in part used for this purpose. Since the closure of Chancery Lane, however, it has become the Map and Large Document Reading Room, where medieval and early modern documents (many of which will not fit on the smaller desks in the main reading room) are produced. The specialist finding-aids for this material are also kept on open shelves here. Because of the nature of the documents produced in this room, and the type of reader who mostly works there, it is beginning to acquire something of the atmosphere of the old Round Room at Chancery Lane, although new readers should not allow themselves to feel intimidated as a result.

Anyone arriving for the first time at a large record office is likely to feel slightly bewildered: the PRO has recognised this at Kew in a way that was never the case at Chancery Lane and has positioned well-trained staff as well as notices and leaflets at strategic points in both the smaller reference room at the top of the stairs on the first floor and the larger room beyond which contains the bulk of the finding-aids. If you have come to the office with some references in mind, culled either from published material or a letter, it may well be best to show your notes or the letter to a member of staff, who will then explain how to find the appropriate class list from which you can identify the exact reference numbers of the documents you wish to see.

The confusing array of lists at Chancery Lane, which seemed to come in all shapes and sizes, printed, typed or hand-written, some as old as the documents to which they related, arranged around the walls of both main reading-rooms and on island bookcases down the side of one of them, which for some readers was all part of the esoteric charm of the place, has been largely swept away at Kew in favour of a much simpler arrangement. The great majority of the class lists, forming a 'standard set', are shelved in alphabetical order of lettercode in the bookcases lining the walls of both the main reference room and the smaller outer room; there are several identical sets of lists available in the two rooms and also in the second-floor reading room. For some classes, mostly older material that used to be at Chancery Lane, there are still some 'non-standard' finding-aids in use, which are kept either in the Map and Large Document Reading Room or on the free-standing bookcases in the main reference room on the first floor, on which will also be found the more detailed indexes available for certain classes in addition to the basic lists. A diagram showing which volumes are shelved where is available in the reference room and, once again, the enquiry staff can help with specific questions.

Also available in the reference room are several sets of the 'Current Guide', which at first sight is a rather forbidding series of binders containing the thousands of pages of text which have replaced the old published *Guide*. It takes a little time to find your way around this work, but essentially it consists of an outline history of each court or department whose records are at the PRO, a more detailed account of each class of records within the different groups, and a very comprehensive index. Finally, in the smaller of the two reference rooms there is a nest of pigeon-holes from which you can help yourself to copies of the office's series of guides to particular classes of record or particular topics (essentially those about which most enquiries are received). Like the Current Guide, the modest format in which they are produced belies the vast amount of authoritative information distilled into these leaflets.

Once you have found precise references (i.e. lettercode, class number and piece number) to at least some of the documents you wish to see, you are almost ready to order the first three items. The one remaining preliminary is to go into the reading room and ask to be allocated a seat, since each seat has a unique number and documents are issued to a specific seat, as well as a named individual. All the seats in the reading room have power-points, although the counter staff group users of laptop computers or dictating machines away from readers relying on traditional pencil and paper. With your seat number you will be given a radio-pager which is bleeped when your documents arrive. Armed with a seat number you return to the reference room and go to one of the computer terminals grouped around the edge of the room, at which you swipe your reader's ticket through a bar-code reader to activate a simple menu which prompts you for your seat number and the references of the documents you wish to order.

The delay in producing documents inevitably varies from day to day and within the day, depending on the number of readers, the number of documents being ordered and the number of staff available to fetch the material from the strong-rooms, although the office tries to keep the waiting time to under 45 minutes. If you have not been bleeped after this period, it is worth querying whether something has gone wrong. If you have consulted the staff before ordering your first documents, you may already have been advised to ask for a seat in the Map and Large Document Reading Room and order documents to be produced there. If you have been given a seat in the main reading-room but the documents you have ordered can only be produced upstairs, you will be bleeped and the staff will explain where your material can be found.

As soon as your first three documents have arrived you can order another three, and then further items as you return those you have finished with. It is therefore a good idea to have a list of references

from which you can order material throughout the day, and the time
spent waiting for your first three documents to arrive can be put to
good use searching the lists in the reference room. The latest time for
ordering documents you wish to see the same day is 4 p.m., although
you can order material for the following day up to 4.15. If you are
visiting the office on two successive days you can ask for documents to
be kept out overnight, so that they will be ready as soon as the reading
room opens at 9.30. Since the office itself opens to the public at 9 a.m.,
there is a useful extra half-hour in which the finding-aids in the
reference room are available.

Once you have a reader's ticket for the office and some idea of what
you wish to see there, you can also save time on future visits by
phoning (or sending a fax or email) the day before, quoting your
reader's ticket number and three specific document references which
the staff will order in advance to be ready when you arrive.

The PRO offers a comprehensive, if rather expensive, range of
copying services for documents in its care, although many are unsuitable for direct photocopying because of their size, format or condition.
Most hard copies are in fact made from microfilm, which is particularly
expensive if new film has to be made first. The service is useful if you
live some distance from the PRO or find it difficult to visit the office,
but once you are at Kew it is generally better to sit there and read the
documents, rather than run up a huge bill for copies which will take
some time to produce and still need deciphering when you get them.

The PRO: some sources for local history

Something should now be said about what to look at at the PRO. As
with a local record office, this obviously depends on what subject you
are pursuing, but let us take the simple case of someone generally
interested in the history of their town or village. Leaving on one side
the medieval records (since the administrative material is mostly
accessible in print and the judicial sources beyond most amateurs), and
those of the State Paper Office, Privy Council and Treasury which have
also been calendared, there are a number of classes relating to the
period 1500-1700 which are well within the grasp of anyone with some
practice in reading secretary hand.

If you have no specific leads to follow, a good class to start with may be E 179, which contains tax assessments from the beginning of the fourteenth century to the end of the seventeenth. The documents are arranged by county and within each county by date. There is a list published by the List & Index Society. This is currently being super-seded by an automated database available at the PRO, which will make it much easier to locate material relating to individual communities, and it is worth asking the staff if your county has been recatalogued in this way. Assuming the material has not been published by the local record society, it is usually worth looking at hearth tax assessments for your parish, since these should provide a fairly complete list of householders for at least one date during the period 1662-88 when the tax was collected. There will be a separate assessment for each hundred within the county, so order the piece for the hundred in which your parish lies. For each parish (or township in the north of England) there will be a list of names of those who paid hearth tax, possibly followed by a list of those who were exempt on the grounds of poverty, plus the number of hearths each householder had in his house. The latter is a rough guide to social standing, and in villages where there was only one large house it should be possible to identify the occupier from the assessment. Names in hearth tax lists can also be linked to probate records, to see whether people with large houses had large inventories. A hearth tax assessment which includes those discharged from payment as well as those charged should include almost every household in the parish. Multiply the number of names by an estimate of average household size (4.75 tends to be the most commonly used) and you have a rough estimate of population to compare with that for 1801 from the first census, or with other estimates derived from pre-census sources. Alternatively, you can avoid the difficulty of which multiplier to choose and simply compare the number of households in the hearth tax assessment with the figure in the first census return.

Hearth tax records come almost at the end of E 179 and it is worth going back over the previous hundred years of the class to look at other documents. Most of these will be assessments to lay subsidies, a tax (to which the clergy were assessed separately, hence the name) levied on men's wealth in goods or land. In the second half of the sixteenth century its imposition became fossilised and fell very lightly on only a few people in each village (sometimes called subsidy men as a mark of social standing), but two subsidies of the reign of Henry VIII are rich sources for the local historian. For southern English counties that of

1524-7 should provide a list of householders in each community, excluding the poorest third of the population who were exempt from the tax. For northern England and Wales (which was only brought into the English tax system in 1536) the subsidy of 1543-7 is likely to be fuller. Returns of this period are harder to read than hearth tax assessments, but anyone with experience of an early parish register should be able to manage a simple list of names and amounts paid. For both lay subsidies and hearth tax, and indeed other contemporary material on population and social structure, there is a large literature on the documents and their interpretation.

The Tudor and Stuart Exchequer was not merely a revenue-collecting department but also a court of law, with a jurisdiction that brought before it many cases of local interest. During this period the Exchequer collected a great deal of evidence in 'depositions', which recorded witnesses' (strictly speaking, deponents') answers to a set of questions put before them by both plaintiff and defendant. These depositions are to be found mainly in two classes (E 134 and E 178) and abound in colourful local detail. The only published list appeared in the nineteenth century and was arranged chronologically for the whole country. Many years ago, someone at the PRO had the good idea of cutting up a copy of this list and putting it back together again county-by-county; no-one has since had the even better idea of printing these volumes. However, once you have found this pasted-up compilation among the 'non-standard' lists and looked up your county, the chances are that there will be at least a couple of cases relating to people or places you are interested in.

Documents in both E 134 and E 178 are written in English in a hand no more difficult than that used for local records of the same period. For each case there will usually be a file of several membranes of parchment, starting with a list of questions ('interrogatories') administered by the plaintiff to his deponents. Then will come the answers, followed by the same sequence for the defendant. Both questions and answers are informal in style and often contain much topographical detail (description of property or boundaries of manors), eye-witness accounts of disputed incidents (riotous assembly or illegal inclosure), and sometimes reported speech (each side accusing the other of making incriminating statements). Depositions can also be a useful source of biographical information, since each witness prefaced his replies by giving his name, place of residence, occupation and age.

Depositions were a preliminary stage in an Exchequer action and it is sometimes possible to trace other documents in the case, following the directions at the front of the list of depositions. Proceedings in several other equity courts in the early modern period follow roughly the same course as in the Exchequer. Those for the Chancery are probably the most accessible, since there are published lists from the middle of the sixteenth century to the middle of the seventeenth. Chancery depositions, however, are not as full as those taken by the Exchequer, although they are also in English rather than Latin. It is worth adding that another project currently in progress at the PRO is the creation of a database that will make it possible to search both the Exchequer and Chancery depositions, and those taken in the smaller equity courts, far more effectively than is the case at present.

The PRO contains large quantities of material generated by Crown ownership of manors and other property, the equivalent of estate collections in local offices. Manorial documents are included in the Manorial Documents Register at the National Register of Archives (p. 61) and so this source can be checked without difficulty. Court rolls and some other cognate material, such as rentals and surveys, were brought together in the past in a group called Special Collections, which is well covered in the old series of published *Lists & Indexes*. Elsewhere in Part I of the 1963 *Guide* will be found details of Crown muniments for estates owned by the Duchy of Lancaster or the palatinates of Chester and Durham, which will be of value to local historians in certain parts of the country. The records of the Duchy of Cornwall remain in the hands of that body.

For all parts of the country it is worth investigating those classes of Exchequer records which once belonged to the Court of Augmentations, set up by Henry VIII to administer confiscated monastic lands. While the wealth of the church on the eve of the Dissolution can be studied in the published *Valor Ecclesiasticus* mentioned earlier (p. 137), the later history of former monastic lands and their disposal by Henry's successors has to be sought from the unprinted Augmentations records, unless a local society has published the material. There is a short account of Augmentations material in the *Guide*, and at the PRO there are a number of manuscript calendars of leases and grants of the lands, from which it may be possible to identify documents tracing the history of an estate in your parish from the 1530s to the mid seventeenth century. Augmentations records also contain material relating to the religious gilds and chantries dissolved by Edward VI, again including leases and grants tracing the later ownership of the property, most of which lay in towns. Finally, the Court of Augmentations, and several other departments, acquired large quantities of deeds for property which passed through Crown hands. The List & Index Society has issued calendars of thousands of these 'ancient deeds', supplementing an older *Catalogue of Ancient Deeds* published by the PRO itself, and all these volumes are obviously worth checking for references to places in which you are interested.

Turning to the PRO's more modern holdings, it will be obvious that many of the most heavily used groups, such as Cabinet Office, Foreign Office or Colonial Office records, or the service departments, contain little or nothing of local interest (although Admiralty, Army and RAF records can be useful for towns with service connections). Some of the records of the more strictly domestic departments contain references to local communities, such as correspondence regarding early nineteenth-century 'disturbances' among the Home Office papers or many of the early files of the Ministry of Labour and Ministry of Transport, but they may not be arranged, or even indexed, by place. Similarly, most of the administrative and financial (as opposed to engineering) records of the pre-1947 railway companies are at the PRO but may be of limited interest to local historians other than those working specifically on transport history. For those seeking to discover more about their community generally, the modern material likely to be of greatest interest are the records of the nineteenth-century departments which supervised the emergence of the modern local government system, whose own records have already been described (pp. 54-9).

Each of the statutory reforms outlined in Chapter 3 involved the setting up of a central department to supervise local elected boards. The pattern established by the Poor Law Amendment Act of 1834 was copied in the Public Health Acts of 1848 and later and the Education Acts of 1870 and 1902. The records of the central department include correspondence with each local authority in the middle decades of the nineteenth century and, for the later period, files containing minutes as well as letters to and from the authority. This material greatly amplifies what can be discovered of local government in a particular parish, including not merely public health reform but also poor relief and education. Even if the board of guardians or the local board records in a county record office include letter-books, it is useful to go to the PRO and look at the central department's files as well, since they may contain comments by civil servants about policy, endorsed on letters from the local authority, and minutes to guide those responsible for drafting replies.

The records of the older ancestors of the Department for Education and Employment—the Education Department of the Privy Council, the Board of Education and the Ministry of Education—are especially useful for the local history of the subject from 1870 onwards. Not merely is there a series of files for each local authority (each school board under the 1870 Act, each county education committee or 'Part III' authority under that of 1902) but an even larger class containing a file for every school that has ever received a grant from central funds, in other words all schools in the maintained sector. This is one area where the modern records of central government reach down to the lowest level, adding to whatever is available in a county record office or at the school itself. These files, and those on the department's dealing with the local authorities, are especially interesting where there was any clash, either between rival local interests, or between the local authority and the central department.

There is a good deal of other material of local interest among the modern classes at the PRO besides those already mentioned, although detailed guidance is beyond the scope of an introductory book and is in any case the main theme of my *Record Sources for Local History*. One more class is perhaps worth picking out, since it tends to be neglected and yet is relatively straightforward to use. If you are interested in the history of any business conducted as a limited liability company, it is worth checking whether the file of returns kept during the company's lifetime by the Companies Registration Office (i.e. Companies House, established in 1844) has survived to reach the PRO (to become class BT 31, apart from some early files, which form BT 41). For a company dissolved before 1920, there are finding-aids at Kew; for companies that survived beyond this date (when the chances of the file being retained actually diminish) it is possible to ask Companies House (Crown Way, Cardiff CF4 3UZ) to search a card index which will provide the PRO reference to any surviving file. If you are interested in an old established company that is still on the register there will be material at Cardiff.

Record keeping since 1066: centre and locality

From this very brief outline of material in the PRO of interest to local historians, or better still from the old *Guide* or *Record Sources*, it should be possible to see how the records of central government relate to those in local record offices and how the two together, for different periods, are more or less useful for local studies. In simple terms, one can divide English history between the Norman Conquest and the First World War into three main periods, each of which has been marked by an increase in record creation and preservation as the machinery of government has become more complex. Thus in the twelfth and thirteenth centuries a system of central administration was established in England which led to the creation of the very fine medieval archives of the Chancery, the Exchequer and the subsidiary courts, which more than a century of publishing and scholarly interpretation have made widely available. Although the Crown in this period imposed its will on the localities through (for the most part) the sheriff of each county, there is no corresponding archive of medieval local public records, and such documents as there are from the Middle Ages in county record offices are essentially private muniments of families, religious houses or chartered boroughs. This material is much less voluminous and much less systematic in character than the central records.

The Tudor revolution in government, from the 1530s onwards, greatly extended the scope of central administration in England, brought Wales within its ambit for the first time, and led to a vast increase in both the creation and preservation of records. At the same time, the first steps were taken to establish a system of local government, with parliament laying certain duties on the justices of each county (or large borough) and the voluntary officials of each parish (or township). It is thus in this period, at least in well documented counties, that the official holdings of county record offices begin, with quarter sessions and parish records supplementing what is available in private collections. Up to 1660, however, central government and the higher courts of law continued to take a close interest in the localities, which is why for this period there remains much of local interest in the PRO. After 1660, and more especially after the revolution of 1688, central government's interference in the day-to-day affairs of local communities receded and did not reassert itself until the early nineteenth century. It is for this reason that the eighteenth-century public records seem less useful for the local historian than those of either the century before or after, although this may also owe something to the paucity of published calendars or finding-aids indexed by place. But it was in this period that the administration of local communities lay largely in their own hands, mainly through the parish or county, and for which the other most important sources for local history are often collections of family and estate papers or business records. Even in the early period of the Industrial Revolution (say 1760-1830) central sources for local history remain limited.

All this was to change later in the nineteenth century as a result of a transformation of government and administration, at both national and local level, more revolutionary than that of the sixteenth century. Between the 1830s and the First World War central government was vastly extended and took a closer interest in local communities—for example through the new departments dealing with poor relief, public health or education—than it had since before 1660. At the same time the system of local administration through the county and parish, established by the Tudors and modified by their successors, was completely overhauled as new institutions were established and existing ones revitalised, creating the local administrative records described in Chapter 3. Private muniments, especially those of landed families, also become much bulkier in the nineteenth century, which is why local record offices have a far larger quantity of both deposited and official records for this period than for any earlier century. Since 1914, especially since 1945, there has in effect been a continuing revolution in government, creating archives on a scale which overshadows even that of the late nineteenth century.

The implications for the local historian of this pattern of record creation, at national and local level in England since the eleventh century, and in Wales since the sixteenth, may be summarised thus. From Domesday Book to the Dissolution (1086–c. 1540) local material is limited in England to private muniments and for most Welsh communities hardly exists; the records of central government contain much relating to localities which is available in print in one form or another. From the mid sixteenth century to the early nineteenth there is a growing bulk of material in local custody; for the first half of this period the enlarged public records contain a great deal of material relating to local communities, whereas after 1700 they become less useful. Finally, from about 1830 to 1914 (and beyond) there is a wealth of records, private and official, in local offices, and much more in the Public Record Office. An overview of this kind may seem irrelevant to beginners who simply wish to trace the history of their house or find out when their great-grandparents were born, but if their interest develops they should appreciate how the pattern of record creation has changed over the centuries, why some periods are better documented than others, and why for some centuries one relies more heavily on the PRO and for others on a local repository.

Family Records Centre

Early in 1997 the PRO and the Office for National Statistics joined forces to open a new Family Records Centre at 1 Myddleton Street, London EC1, which lies within reasonable walking distance of Angel, Farringdon and King's Cross St Pancras Underground stations, is close to the London Metropolitan Archives (the former Greater London Records Office) and not far from the Society of Genealogists' headquarters. The centre has the indexes of births, marriages and deaths and other indexes previously made available at St Catherine's House by the former Office of Population Censuses and Surveys (which itself absorbed the General Register Office some years before), and also the most heavily used genealogical sources which used to be accessible at the Chancery Lane branch of the PRO. These include the census enumerators' books for 1841-91 for the whole of England and Wales (p. 35), the Estate Duty Office registers and indexes, the registered wills and administrations of the Prerogative Court of Canterbury up to 1858 (p. 70; these are also available at Kew) and the Nonconformist registers of birth, baptism, marriage and burial which were surrendered to the Registrar General in the mid nineteenth century. As already explained (p. 72), the FRC also has indexes to wills proved throughout England and Wales since 1858, but the wills themselves are kept elsewhere in London.

The centre has broadly the same opening hours as the PRO, including late evenings on Tuesday and Thursday, and is also open for the whole of Saturday. There is an information and sales point, a refreshment area and both self-service and staffed photocopying for the census and wills. Since it opened, it has become an extremely valuable facility for those who wish to conduct genealogical research over the whole of England and Wales from a central London base, and a far more comfortable place at which to work than either St Catherine's House or Chancery Lane.

British Library Department of Manuscripts

Apart from the PRO, one of the other national institutions which local historians come across at an early stage in their studies is the Department of Manuscripts of the British Library, formerly the British Museum and thus cited in the footnotes to older works as 'B.M.'. As this book goes to press, the department is closed to readers and in the process of moving from its old home at the British Museum in Great Russell Street to the new British Library near St Pancras Station, so that it is impossible to describe precisely what arrangements for readers will be when it reopens. Assuming they remain broadly unchanged, however, admission to the new reading room will be by ticket, for which one should make written application in advance. In the past this has been forthcoming without difficulty if you are working on a topic which requires the resources of the department, or have references to particular documents in the collection, whereas access to the printed books department of the British Library (already open at St Pancras), for which a separate reader's ticket is required, is more narrowly restricted to those who cannot readily obtain the books they need elsewhere.

The manuscript collections of the British Library are rather different in character from those of either the PRO or a local repository. Although there are a few administrative records in the BL, the bulk of the collection is essentially 'private', consisting of the personal or political papers of statesmen, soldiers, sailors and the like; literary and musical manuscripts; and historical and antiquarian collections. The last category, which is likely to be of most interest to local historians, has brought into the library large quantities of medieval documents, especially the cartularies (manuscript volumes into which title deeds were copied) of religious houses, which were salvaged by antiquaries after the Dissolution. As well as manuscripts, there is also a large collection of mostly medieval charters (normally written in Latin) relating to lands in every county in England. These have often been included in nineteenth-century published calendars (which give detailed summaries in English), although the collection has been added to since most such books were published, while modern practice is to include more topographical detail from medieval deeds than was the case a century ago.

The system of references and finding-aids at the BL also differs from that at the PRO or a local record office. In the first place, almost all manuscripts either arrive as bound volumes or are made up into volumes at the library. Except in the case of charters, a reader is normally presented with a volume, rather than a box of loose documents or individual items. Most of the deeds form a series called simply 'Additional Charters', followed by a serial number, although there are some smaller sequences, such as the Egerton Charters, with their own numbering. A similar plan is followed with the manuscripts. Whereas in a local record office the papers of (say) Sir Robert Peel would have been given a separate deposit number or mnemonic abbreviation, in the British Museum they were simply bound up into volumes and given the next block of numbers in the Additional Manuscripts series. The term 'Additional' (as in Add.Ch. or Add.MS. in footnotes) implies that some other material was there in the first place. These are the Harleian Manuscripts (and a smaller collection of Harleian Charters) assembled by Robert Harley, whose magnificent collection of medieval and later manuscripts form one of the nuclei around which the rest of the collection has been built since 1753. The Harleian Manuscripts are an especially rich source for heraldry and genealogy, and often the first reference to a BL document many local historians come across will be a copy of a herald's visitation for their county in this collection.

There is an impressive and reasonably straightforward set of catalogues to the BL manuscript collection, which is available in most university and larger public libraries. A catalogue of the Harleian Manuscripts was published by the Record Commission in the early nineteenth century, followed by a similar publication by the Trustees of the British Museum for the first group of Additional Manuscripts. The Museum issued further catalogues over the following century, a process continued by the British Library. These describe each volume of Additional or other manuscripts in numerical order (and also the various series of charters) and each is indexed. More useful, however, is the consolidated index to the entire run of published catalogues now available. If you are tracing the history of a parish, or looking for some fairly well known individual, and can find a copy of these index volumes, it takes only a few minutes to make a search under the name of the place or person you are interested in and then go to the appropriate volume of the catalogue to find a description of the manuscript. If you are unable to visit the library to follow up the reference in person, the department can supply copies in various formats, most commonly microfilm or a print made from film.

A search for a particular place in the BL catalogues may well reveal a block of Additional Manuscripts which form antiquarian collections for your county. Since there were no local record offices until the early twentieth century and no public libraries until the late nineteenth, the papers of older antiquaries have sometimes ended up in the BL, even though their scope is entirely local. In a few cases local studies libraries have acquired the material on microfilm, otherwise it is available only in London and may not be catalogued in as much detail as a local historian might like. The older collections for a county history, now most commonly in the British Library or the Bodleian Library (p. 155), are generally much more valuable (whether or not the work was eventually published) than the more recent material of the same sort found in local libraries (pp. 34-5). There may well be extensive genealogical notes for a large number of families, including drawings of coats of arms; an antiquary may have made careful ink and wash sketches of local churches before Victorian rebuilding, or views of field monuments now much altered. Unpublished collections assembled by the major historian of your county may be relatively well known, but material belonging to lesser antiquaries may hardly have been used. One collection of general interest is that containing the papers of Daniel and Samuel Lysons, the promoters of the abortive *Magna Britannia* project of the early nineteenth century (pp. 11-12), covering not only the counties for which volumes were published, but also those alphabetically beyond Devon for which nothing appeared. They include both notes from records and correspondence with local clergy in search of information.

Another class of material for which the BL has long been well known are heralds' visitations, the books compiled by officers of the College of Arms during tours of the counties in the sixteenth and seventeenth centuries. These contain not merely the arms and pedigrees of gentle families but often also notes on heraldic decoration in domestic buildings and churches and on church monuments. Most of the official visitation records are at the College of Arms but because of their antiquarian interest the books were widely pirated and dozens of copies, usually inferior to those at the college, exist in the Harleian Manuscripts and elsewhere. In the late nineteenth century it was popular to publish visitations for particular counties and this became the main activity of the Harleian Society, which still undertakes such work. Most nineteenth-century editions of visitations are inaccurate transcripts of poor copies, especially those published other than by the Harleian Society, and there have been few scholarly modern editions (perhaps a sign of changing antiquarian taste). In counties with a large-scale published history the substance of visitation pedigrees will usually appear in the accounts of families whose arms were recorded, or there may be an edition, good or bad, of a visitation for your county published separately. If neither is the case, and you are interested in a family whose arms and pedigree were recorded by the heralds, it may be worth looking at visitation books in the British Library or elsewhere.

College of Arms

The most authoritative source of information on heraldic matters is, of course, still the College of Arms, which can be found in an attractive seventeenth-century building in Queen Victoria Street, on the edge of the City. As well as the main collection of visitation books the college also houses its own records, the papers of many past officers of arms, a fine reference library, and a considerable quantity of more general antiquarian collections relating to most parts of the country. There is a brief published guide. Traditionally, the College of Arms was reluctant to allow searchers to use its collections directly and one had to work, at some expense, through one of the officers. While it remains a private, rather than public repository, most users would probably agree that there has been a distinct change in atmosphere at the college in the last twenty years. Local historians who wish to pursue some enquiry there, preferably not directly heraldic or genealogical, will find the Registrar & Librarian (who is also a herald) helpful and co-operative. Members of the college naturally still charge for their services in tracing pedigrees or making applications for grants of arms, many of them these days for corporate clients, although it seems unlikely that they have benefited from the upsurge of interest in genealogy of recent years to anything like the same extent as did their late Victorian predecessors during the last such revival.

Bodleian Library and Cambridge University Library

Local historians particularly interested in antiquarian papers will probably also wish to explore two other national repositories, both of which have substantial manuscript collections, the Bodleian being especially rich in topographical material, not merely for Bucks., Berks. and Oxon. but for the whole country. The published finding-aids for the two university libraries are not widely available but one can obviously follow up specific references by correspondence and, if there is something you wish to look at, ask for a reader's ticket or order copies. Both libraries, it should be noted, have transferred their former function as diocesan record offices to the Oxfordshire and Cambridgeshire county record offices.

Local historians tracing the history of landed estates may come across property owned by one of the Oxford or Cambridge colleges, in which case it is worth writing to the archivist of the college concerned to see what estate records survive, which may still be at the college or may have been deposited at the Bodleian or the UL. If you are simply interested in the career of a former member of a college (most commonly a local parson) it is generally not worth contacting the college: there are published lists of members of both universities from the middle ages to the late nineteenth century available in large public libraries and only in the case of particularly well known graduates will the college library or archives have any further information.

House of Lords Record Office

Most local historians probably first encounter the House of Lords Record Office through an interest in transport history, since among its holdings are the proceedings before the parliamentary committees which examined canal and railway bills. Virtually all the records of the House of Commons were destroyed by fire in 1834, but those of the Lords include unpublished minutes recording the investigation by committees of the house into local bills of this sort (including later in the nineteenth century schemes for docks, street tramways and electricity undertakings, as well as the better known canal and railway projects). Like the plans deposited with clerks of the peace for such schemes (pp. 106-7), of which there will be another copy at the House of Lords if the project went ahead, these committees include many concerned with bills which were ultimately unsuccessful. For anyone pursuing the history of transport in their area, they are a useful source, since witnesses went into considerable detail about trade and the likely benefits from a particular project, and sometimes discussed the fortunes of their own business.

There is no published list of canal and railway committee minutes in the House of Lords and in the past the best way to identify material was to follow a scheme through Parliament, from its formal first reading to its abandonment or royal assent. The intricacies of eighteenth- and nineteenth-century local bill procedure are too complicated to explain here but with a little practice can be grasped from the *Journals* of the two Houses of Parliament. These can be found in larger reference libraries and for the eighteenth century will contain the substance of any petitions sent in for or against a bill, which are often extremely useful, if partisan, comments on the pattern of local trade. One then had to write to the House of Lords Record Office to see what unpublished papers, if any, survive from the committee stage. Recently, however, the accessibility of committee papers, especially for topics other than transport history, has been greatly enhanced by the compilation of an automated database in which searches can be made for individuals and also those engaged in particular industries (details available from the HLRO).

Local bills were not debated on the floor of either House and so are not referred to in the published *Parliamentary Debates* (Hansard), which form the almost verbatim records of proceedings, whereas the *Journals* are in the nature of minute books, merely recording decisions. The House of Lords is not the place to go simply to read the *Journals* or to explore the immense wealth of published nineteenth-century Parliamentary Papers (alias Sessional Papers, Blue Books, Royal Commissions, Select Committees etc.). This material needs a book of its own to explain and several have been published. Complete sets of Parliamentary Papers exist in only a handful of national libraries but some major reference libraries have good collections and the principal university libraries have the standard microfiche edition of the entire set (as does the PRO), from which prints of individual pages can be made. Some of the better known Victorian reports were reprinted some years ago by an Irish publisher (in a distinctive green leather binding) and these are also quite widely available.

Printed sets of Acts of Parliament can also be found in public and university libraries, although the more familiar series of Public and General Acts do not contain those relating to canals, railways, gasworks and the like, or those promoted in the late nineteenth century by local authorities (both of which categories are known as Local and Personal Acts), or those dealing with inclosure or the affairs of individuals or families (Private Acts). For the nineteenth century these were published in separate series, which are much less widely available, although copies of individual Acts relating to a particular town can often be found in the appropriate local studies library, or in the county record office, which may have taken over the law library assembled by former clerks of the peace. In case of difficulty, the House of Lords Record Office can supply photocopies.

Church records

The structure of record keeping in the Church of England at diocesan level and below has already been described (pp. 52; cf. 158-9 for Wales). The provincial records for the northern province (including probate records) are kept at the Borthwick Institute of the University of York, while those for the southern province (apart from those of the Prerogative Court of Canterbury, for which see p. 150) are divided between Lambeth Palace Library and the Centre for Kentish Studies (i.e. the county and diocesan record office) at Maidstone. More recently, a Church of England Records Centre has been established in London to accommodate and make more easily available the modern (i.e. post-1704) records of several central organisations, including those of the National Society (i.e. the Church's educational work), and the Ecclesiastical Commissioners and Queen Anne's Bounty (whose functions are now combined in the work of the Church Commissioners). The first of these groups is always worth checking if you are interested in the history of a village school that was founded as a National (i.e. Church of England) school, since there should be a file on every school that has ever received financial aid from the National Society. The second is mainly concerned (at parish level) with the endowments and income of each benefice, or with parsonage houses and their upkeep, and is thus of more limited interest, although still worth consulting for the detailed history of a parish church.

If you are pursuing the history of a Nonconformist congregation it is always worth starting with the resources of the local studies library or county record office, although you may find the results searches there disappointing. This is partly because the survival of chapel records is much poorer compared to those of the established church, but also because some denominations have a policy of collecting material into a central repository. Among the older churches this is particularly true of the Society of Friends (Quakers), most of whose records are kept at Friends' House, Euston Road, London. Similarly, the Methodists, although not opposed to local deposit, have created a Connexional Archive at the John Rylands Library, which is part of Manchester University. Stephens's *Sources for English Local History* provides a thorough guide to this complex subject, which is beyond the scope of an introductory book.

The Roman Catholic Church in England and Wales does not deposit material in local record offices, nor does it maintain a central repository. Each diocese is responsible for its own records and arrangements for access vary considerably. Parish records remain in the custody of parishes.

National Library of Wales

Since this book is aimed at local historians in Wales as well as England, it would be wrong not to mention the National Library at Aberystwyth. As well as a department of printed books which acts as the copyright library for Wales, the library has a department of manuscripts and records which is in some respects analogous to the equivalent British Library department, but also houses some Welsh public records transferred from the PRO and has a range of deposited private muniments which make it comparable to a particularly well endowed county record office in England. A comprehensive guide to the department has recently been published.

The major group of public records at the National Library are the papers of the court of Great Sessions of Wales, established in 1542, which until its abolition in 1830 occupied a position broadly equivalent to that of the assize courts in England, although the records are better preserved than those of most assize circuits. The library also has the diocesan and other non-parochial records of the Church in Wales, including the probate records of the four ancient Welsh dioceses; Welsh parish registers are divided between the NLW and local record offices. In addition, there are extensive collections of Welsh Nonconformist records at Aberystwyth, particularly for Welsh Presbyterian congregations. The other great strength of the manuscript department is in estate papers, especially collections from estates broken up by sale before 1939, when there were few local record offices in Wales.

The library also has a department of pictures and maps, which is of enormous value to local historians in Wales, since it not only has the largest collection of both Ordnance Survey and estate maps anywhere in the principality, and the diocesan copies of Welsh tithe maps, but, equally important, first class copying facilities unrivalled by those of any local record office. Its collection of prints, drawings and photographs (to which have been added in recent years ciné films and videos) is another invaluable resource, although it is worth mentioning that several branches of the National Museums & Galleries of Wales (especially the Museum of Welsh Life at St Fagans near Cardiff) also have large photographic collections.

CHAPTER SEVEN

Writing and Publication

Publishing is important

This chapter concerns two topics to which beginners rarely give much thought and which most amateurs never do anything about. It is, unfortunately, only too easy to carry on collecting information, possibly for years, without taking any steps to write up your discoveries, whether you are simply working for your own amusement or are supposed to be preparing a higher degree dissertation. Part-time amateur enthusiasts do not even have the inducement of a degree at the end of the day or the pressure of a supervisor to get on and write something, and may take the view that they have nothing to say of interest to anyone except themselves. It may be that the history of one's own family will be of little interest to anyone other than family members, but in most other cases any piece of work done with reasonable care and thoroughness will be of some interest to someone somewhere, if they know about it. Even an account of your house may make a short article for a local magazine.

False modesty has some charm; a more irritating trait is the refusal to publish anything for fear of letting others know of your discoveries. It is a mark of the worst kind of antiquarianism to regard knowledge as a species of private property and to refuse to talk about and share your research with others. It is also usually counter-productive, since publication can often stimulate new discoveries and even a talk to a local audience can encourage others to pass on information. Another excuse for never publishing anything is that you haven't finished. This is also bogus. Research is never finished—that is not how historical knowledge works—but all local historians get to a point where they have something to say, even if all the loose ends have not been tied up and you may wish to write a fuller account of the same topic five years later. The accumulation of antiquarian notes in most libraries referred to in Chapter 2 (pp. 34-5) should be a sufficient warning against never writing anything, at least for those local historians who really do want to be more than aimless antiquaries.

Local historians who never write anything may claim that they are waiting until they have completed the history of their parish before producing one large book on their life's work. This is again an unsound basis on which to proceed. Apart from the likelihood of dying or losing interest before you have finished the definitive history of anywhere, you will almost certainly find that the complete history of a parish is unpublishably long, mainly for financial reasons; it will probably be utterly unreadable too. It is very difficult to write a consistently interesting village history from Domesday Book to the Great War, for reasons that should have become clear in the chapters on source material. All local historians soon come across the sort of parish history, so popular between about 1870 and 1914 but by no means extinct today, which begins with the complete (usually untranslated and unexplained) text of the relevant entry in Domesday Book, followed after a couple of pages on the Black Death in England by a transcript of the first parish register, commencing in 1558. Apart from a manorial descent lifted from the county history, most chapters on the Middle Ages in a book like this contain little of substance and nothing of interest.

It is a basic sign of weakness in any historical writing to let the material dominate the narrative, although this still happens in so many village histories. There will be virtually nothing on the medieval period, then a great wad of inaccurately transcribed probate inventories, wills and churchwardens' accounts, followed by another gap for the eighteenth century, perhaps punctuated by some quarter sessions material from a published calendar. Nine-tenths of the book will be devoted to the period after 1800, especially those years with magnetic attraction for the village antiquary: 1851, 1861, 1871 and so on. The book usually concludes with the author's own recollections of the village fifty years ago, the work of the Home Guard during the last war, and pictures of the Coronation of 1953 and Silver Jubilee of 1977, which were probably marked by planting either a tree or a new seat on the village green.

If a history of this kind succeeds in getting into print, either because of the personal wealth of the author or the misguided generosity of the parish council, it will be bought eagerly by the 500 or so subscribers whose names will be printed at the back (where the unsuspecting might have looked for an index, which these books never have). The happy purchasers will hurry home with their autographed copy (50p extra for church funds), open the book at Chapter 1, find themselves baffled by the misspelt geological terms, misunderstood archaeological discoveries and out-of-date early medieval history subsumed under the heading 'From the earliest times to the Norman Conquest' and put the book away, never to pick it up again. Local history will thus have lost another 500 sympathetic readers.

Books like this do still get published, especially in the wealthier parts of the country, despite all the advice given to amateur local historians about what to write and how to present their information. If you are interested in the general history of your parish—and there is nothing wrong with this in itself—rather than in some thematic topic, do not think in terms of producing a complete village history in one large, handsomely printed and bound volume. Even if you live long enough to finish it and have the money to publish it, the result is still likely to be very boring. There are many better ways of both writing and publishing local history.

Writing an article

The approach of the competent amateur towards publication is usually rather different from that of the professional, or would-be academic. The latter frequently tries to disguise articles on local topics, which after all do not take as much time or effort to write as those on general problems, with grandiose titles, especially when submitting them to the more prestigious journals. Thus 'New light on rural depopulation in the later Middle Ages' will actually be based on one set of manor court rolls, but with a title like that it has a fair chance of getting into *Past and Present*, if not the *Economic History Review*, whereas 'The manor of Barset, 1350-1500', which may be just as thorough an analysis of the same documents (it may even be virtually the same article) sounds from the start as if it is destined for the *Barsetshire Archaeological Journal*. This is an affectation not to be copied by the experienced amateur whose work may well be of a comparable standard to that of many higher degree students. Local work is best published in local journals where local people will read it, where it will be listed in national bibliographies read by scholars looking for case-studies to illuminate general questions.

The top tier of local publishing has for a long time been occupied by the county journals (pp. 12-13). These are now generally edited to a high standard and mostly publish a combination of archaeological reports, for which substantial subsidies can be collected, and historical articles, which usually have to be financed entirely by the publishing society. The journals normally appear annually and are distributed to the society's members, whose numbers will probably be between 500 and 2,000, depending on the wealth of the county, the length of time the society has been established and the vigour of its committee. County journals are also subscribed to by most university libraries and articles in them are guaranteed a good circulation in this country and abroad. A more recent development has been the publication of three 'regional' history journals, *Northern History, Southern History* and *Midland History*. By contrast with these newer periodicals, the county journals may seem old-fashioned, but they have been around for a long time and remain a good outlet for local historians doing worthwhile work on their area.

Beginners reading this book are probably not thinking of sending an article to the county journal, nor of offering to edit a volume for the local record society, which in some counties shares the 'heavy' end of local history publishing with the archaeological society. Just because they do not see themselves in these terms does not mean that there will be no suitable outlet for their work. Most county societies, or alternatively some other body such as a federation of village local history groups, publish a magazine which solicits, indeed is frequently desperate for, contributions on a more modest scale than those sought by the editor of the county journal. These publications, which tend to go under names like *Loamshire Historian* or *Barsetshire Miscellany*, will probably be quite modest in appearance, printed from text set on a home computer, perhaps with limited facilities for the reproduction of illustrations (although as the hardware and software required for good quality computer graphics become progressively cheaper, this is steadily ceasing to be the case).

The most important point about these magazines is that they are designed as an outlet for the main run of amateur local history, not for substantial county journal length articles or the fourth best chapter of someone's thesis. They will not usually be interested in a complete history of your village, especially if it would have to be printed in 24 instalments, but would welcome a few thousand words, preferably with illustrations, on a local ironworks which you have been studying, or a short account of a village school. The editor will also prefer the article to be submitted in typescript with some indication of sources used, but otherwise these magazines have few pretensions to scholarship. They are a vehicle for amateur work which will interest their two or three hundred readers, and they occasionally publish an article which attracts wider attention. They are the best place for a beginner who has completed some modest project to seek publication, not least because they do not normally involve the author in any financial risk or effort beyond submitting a typescript. Before looking at local history publications that involve both, it may be useful to say something about how to tackle a short article for a local journal.

Some of the most important advice about writing local history was given in the chapter on starting research (pp. 23-9). If you are going to make anything out of your work later it is vital to keep a note of sources, whether in a library or record office. It is also essential, certainly with a project that is going to last any length of time, to order your notes in a coherent manner, probably by subject, so that when you come to write up you can find all the material on a particular topic in one place, preferably in chronological order, from which you can then draft an article, pamphlet or whatever.

As far as actual writing is concerned, it is impossible to say more in a book about local history than appears in any book on English composition. Most people, once they have been out of full-time education for any length of time, and unless they are journalists or have occasion to write continuous prose in the course of their job, find writing difficult. You can read books on English usage, on how to write essays, on how to write well, on how to write clearly. They should all help, but you will probably still find writing a short article very much harder than collecting material for it. This is precisely why it is better to start in a modest way with a piece on one particular topic. Otherwise you are unlikely ever to start, unless forced to do so by, for example, the requirements of a university course, for which a dissertation, typically of 8,000 words or more, will probably be needed at the end of the second or third year. This is of course why the old-fashioned village antiquary never writes anything, or in the end simply cobbles together his notes and transcripts and calls that a parish history. One folder of notes on a single subject is very much easier to make something of than an accumulation of many years divided between several boxes.

Footnotes and references

Where some more specific advice is often welcomed by beginners is in the citation of sources. As the chapters on libraries and record offices explained, there is nothing mysterious about how to cite either printed works or manuscripts. For books and articles you give the normal bibliographical details (author, title etc.) which you should have written at the head of your notes, plus a page reference, unless you are citing the work as a whole. It is for this purpose, as well as to enable the reader to check back to the source, that notes taken from a published work should include the page number. For manuscripts you normally cite the call-number given the document by the record office in which it is kept, prefaced by the name of the repository. In an article where documents are repeatedly cited from the same office, it is usual to shorten the name of the office in second and subsequent references, or give a list of abbreviations at the start of the footnotes. In practice, most readers of *Barsetshire Miscellany* will know what 'BRO' means, although the editor of the *Barsetshire Arch. Journal* will want '(hereafter BRO)' after the full name of the office in the first reference. While most documents in local record offices have alphanumeric reference numbers it is sometimes more help to readers to say what the document actually is, so that they can judge how reliable a source it is. Thus, 'BRO, D801, PI/2' may be enough for an archivist to realise that a parish register is being cited, but for the average reader it is simpler to say this in the footnote.

The beginner writing an article for a local magazine and using footnote references for the first time should avoid picking up certain bad habits found in much pseudo-academic local history. In the case of references to published work it is no longer a sign of scholarship to use *op.cit., loc.cit.* and their friends mentioned earlier (pp. 27-8); they are mostly long overdue for retirement. The standard county history should be cited as J. Smith, *History and Antiquities of the County of Barset* (1791), III, p. 191, on its first appearance, then as Smith, *Barsetshire*, III, p. 200 the next time. The Revd J.J. Smith's article on 'Barsetshire monumental effigies of the later 15th century', *Barsetshire Arch. Journal*, XII (1886), 1-65, may be cited thus if you are mentioning it for the first time *and* want to refer to the whole article (otherwise you would give a specific page number as the last element in the reference); if one particular tomb is referred to later on it can come down to Smith,

'Monumental effigies', p. 32. If you are citing several different articles from the county journal, *BAJ* will probably be intelligible to your local readers after an initial reference in full. If you have two successive references to the same work and the first note cites only one title, it is still convenient to use 'Ibid.' ('the same') in the second; this becomes ambiguous if there is more than one reference in the first note, although 'Ibid.; cf. also ... ' is permissible in the second. Ibid., which is not usually italicised these days, should not be used in a succession of manuscript references.

Another bad habit, known to all examiners of M.A. theses and most book reviewers, is the device of the 'transparent secondary source'. There is nothing necessarily wrong in relying on a statement in a published book, as long as you say honestly where the information is from, and in practice someone writing for *Barsetshire Miscellany* is unlikely to go to the PRO to check that the author of a parish history in VCH has given the figures correctly from the 1670 hearth tax assessment for your parish. What is wrong is not to copy a statement of the number of taxpayers from VCH but to copy the PRO call-number from the footnote in VCH and put that in your reference. In many cases this will look obviously bogus, especially if you transcribe the details incorrectly. If you have used a secondary source, cite the secondary source, not the primary source in the other author's own reference.

One final piece of advice about footnotes, given to all higher degree students, is just as applicable to local historians: use references to tell the reader where you have got a piece of information from, not to continue the text of the article at the bottom of the page or at the end. Some footnotes will obviously have a comment in them beyond a mere title or reference, such as 'I am indebted to Mr J. Smith for help in reading this document' or 'This parish was in Loamshire until 1889 when the county boundary was moved', but do not use a footnote to go off at a tangent. It is also usually unwise either to criticise the work of other local historians, especially if you are likely to meet them in the future, or to give hostages to fortune as to your future intentions, particularly as in sententious phrases like, 'I propose to consider this important question in a future paper' or, worse still, 'This problem will be fully discussed in my forthcoming book'. This exposes you to unsolicited phone calls from complete strangers many years later who have been trying to track down publications you never actually completed.

This advice about how to compose a neatly turned footnote may miss the point that many beginners simply want to be told where to put the damn things in the first place. In articles intended for fairly modest magazines it is in fact often possible to avoid using them at all and much simpler, in work based on only a few sources, to rely on references worked into the text. 'According to Smith (*Barsetshire*, III, p. 191) ... ' or 'A rental of 1735 now in the Barsetshire Record Office (D967/E45) reveals that ... ' is likely to be perfectly acceptable in *Barsetshire Miscellany* and is just as clear as a statement in the text supported by a footnote containing the same information, which is what the *Barsetshire Arch. Journal* will prefer. This technique is halfway towards the method of citation used in scientific publication (including archaeology, although not always in local journals) known as the author-date (or Harvard) system, in which the county history would be cited as 'Smith 1791' in the text and at the end of the article would appear in a list of sources as 'Smith, J. 1791. *History and Antiquities of the County of Barset*'. If you are using conventional footnotes, try to keep the reference numbers to a minimum, especially if the magazine does not use proper index numbers but puts them in brackets. If possible, keep them to the end of sentences, where they least disrupt the text. Thus the statement that 'John Smith was tenant of Townend Farm in 1735, 1741 and 1750, but had left by 1760' can be supported by one reference to four rentals or leases; there is no need to put an index number after each date.

Any precise statement such as this should have a reference; what is not necessary is to support general observations. Readers of 'The Barsetshire Yeomanry in France, 1914-16' will take your word for it that the First World War broke out in August 1914 but will appreciate a reference to a newspaper article describing the Barsetshires' departure for the front, on which you have relied heavily for local detail.

With this simple advice, local historians should be able to compose and annotate a short article on a limited topic for a magazine published by one of the societies in their area. If you are in doubt as to the standard expected, there will be copies of the magazine in the local library which will indicate the sort of contributions included. Even if you have only put together notes on the history of your house, or the development of your suburb as revealed in a sequence of maps, it is worth writing up your finding to bring the work to a conclusion and to pass on information to others.

Illustrations and maps

The editor to whom you submit a piece such as this may well ask for illustrations, since almost all local history magazines can now reproduce half-tone photographs as well as maps and line drawings reasonably successfully. The county journals have all converted to production methods that accommodate half-tones and text on the same page, whereas in the past editors kept plates to the minimum because of the extra expense.

It is not usually very difficult to find some illustrations for almost any local article: either go out and take a couple of clear black and white photographs yourself, or have an old photograph, or an engraving or some other picture copied. What most people find much harder, and frequently duck out of doing to the detriment of the piece of work as a whole, is to provide a map. Most articles in local history magazines, indeed most published local history, would benefit from the inclusion of more maps. Sometimes it is possible to reproduce an old map directly: the earlier editions of the Ordnance Survey can be copied without technical or legal difficulties. More often, however, what is needed is a simple line-drawn sketch map, usually based on an out of copyright OS sheet, which marks the features specifically mentioned in the article rather than the landscape as a whole. It is beyond the scope of this book to give detailed advice on how to draw such maps but there is at least one textbook (admittedly now out-of-date in some respects) which suggests how it is possible to produce acceptable results with simple equipment and no particular artistic skill. Like writing footnotes, there is nothing complicated about producing maps for local history and they greatly improve almost any piece of work. They do not normally add to the cost of publication, since a page of line drawing and a page of text are usually charged for at the same rate by printers.

Books: an introduction to self-publishing

Beginners whose first venture into local history publishing is perhaps to send a six-page article to *Barsetshire Miscellany* on their village school will probably not be greatly concerned about, or knowledgeable of, the cost of getting magazines such as this into print. They will certainly not be concerned with the economics of publishing a parish history of 160 pages or a 96-page book of old photographs. The economics of journal publishing are, however, an obsessive concern of all committees of the larger societies, whose editors and treasurers struggle on from year to year looking for cheaper printers, another source of grant-aid, or occasionally more members. A 36-page stapled magazine reproduced from pages composed at home is not usually confronted with similar problems. As you become more ambitious, however, or become involved in a local group which either publishes a magazine of its own or is seeking to publish something, you may find yourself involved in discussions about printing, publishing and finance.

Despite the unprecedented popular interest in the subject, it remains true, as it always has been, that few mainstream publishers are interested in local history. This is partly because most amateur village histories are so unreadable and partly because their appeal is really so limited. Even with modern printing techniques, which make short-run bookwork more economic than it used to be, a village history of say 200 pages selling perhaps 700 copies out of a printing of 1,000 is not going to appeal to such a publisher. The small number of firms that do claim to be interested in getting amateur parish histories into print usually offer to do so on terms more advantageous to the publisher than the author, or invite prospective readers (or the author, or both) to part with money some months before they receive a book. If you have £3,000 to sink into your life's work on the history of your village and are not too worried as to whether you get the money back, you may as well deal directly with a printer and not put money into the hands of a little known publisher.

Similar advice applies to groups seeking to publish a town or village history. It is usually better to raise the money yourselves, find a competent local printer, get the book published and sell it yourselves. Most of the sales will be to local people and with group effort it is usually possible to get rid of enough copies to break even. This may seem optimistic advice for a newly formed group, attracted but at the same time daunted by the prospect of writing a collaborative history of their town or village, but experience from many parts of the country suggests this is the best way of proceeding. So much work of this kind is now being published that a new group should be able to look at what has been produced recently in its own area and choose a printer, preferably one fairly close at hand, who will turn out an attractive piece of work.

Some readers may feel that this advice is unfair to small specialist publishers with whom they have had successful dealings and seen their work produced to their satisfaction. It is certainly possible to find such firms, although difficult to give detailed advice on the subject, since there tends to be a high mortality rate at this end of the industry and a company that everyone thinks is wonderful one year may, a couple of years later, be no more than a distasteful memory among those who were bitterly disappointed when they saw how their book had come out, or never saw any royalties (or both). It is obviously unwise to name individual publishers here and probably the best advice one can give to anyone thinking of dealing with a such a company is to look at a number of books they have already produced and speak to their authors before committing your book (much less any of your money) into their hands.

It is possible to give more specific advice to those seriously interested in self-publishing. If you are thinking of a full-length book conventionally printed it is not usually worth producing fewer than 500 copies and rarely feasible to consider more than 2,000. Hardback binding with a dust jacket does not add greatly to the cost and does add to both the durability and saleability of the book. Reproducing the text from copy printed on a laser-printer or similar equipment, rather than a professional image-setter, may save money, although not as much as is sometimes supposed, but it will certainly deter some potential customers. A convenient halfway house may well be to give the printer the text on disc for them to output the final ('camera-ready') copy: this is where careful discussion with the printer at an early stage pays off, so that you can let them (or a typesetting bureau) have your text in a format that is compatible with the equipment at their end and so avoid the need to manipulate files, since this will increase costs and may lead to the introduction of errors. Illustrations are vital and the preparation of decent maps time-consuming but essential for a book intended to be of more than antiquarian interest. Here it should be noted that small flatbed scanners sold for general office use will not produce graphics files of sufficiently fine resolution to capture photographs so as to produce an acceptable result on the printed page: give the work to a bureau with the proper equipment.

A more important point, now that most local historians seem to have access to relatively powerful computers, is that neither wordprocessors, nor the software misleadingly known as 'desk-top publishers', will actually design a book for you. (I have yet to meet a desk-top capable of driving round on a wet Saturday afternoon with a car full of books trying to persuade sceptical bookshops to buy them, which is what local history publishing often comes down to.) Such packages may offer various ready-made layouts ('templates') but these tend to be more suitable for sales leaflets or newsletters than books. The better ones will certainly have a remarkably wide range of sophisticated features, some of them using terms (e.g. 'kerning') not widely understood outside the printing industry, or offering options which sound deceptively simple (such as adjusting the space between letters, words or lines of type) but which actually affect the appearance of the finished page in a way that students on degree-level typography courses spend years mastering. The advent of 'Everyman his own Typographer' has done little or nothing for the standard of book design, in both local history and other fields, and anyone who wants their work to come out looking half decent would be well advised either to use a professional typesetting bureau or at least read something about the basic principles of book design. These have, after all, hardly changed over the last four hundred years and still owe more to medieval scribes working before the advent of printing than the latest generation of computer software.

Irrespective of who designs the book and sets the type, getting the book through the press is the printer's job; having the funds to pay the printer and then being able to sell enough copies to recover your outlay are tasks which fall to the local group which decides to act as its own publisher. Raising money seems to frighten such groups more than is necessary. It may still be possible, in the more remote parts of the country into which changing fashions in public expenditure have yet to penetrate, that a grant will be forthcoming from the local council, although this is far less likely than when the first edition of this book was published. Nor is it possible at present to obtain funds from the National Lottery to support local history publishing. The whole range of fund-raising activities favoured by voluntary organisations (car-boot sales, coffee mornings, wine and cheese parties etc.) can be called into play. One can try selling the book in advance on subscription, although this rarely succeeds in raising all the money needed. Another method, which seems not to be used as much as it might be, is simply for the members of the group themselves to pool their own resources and guarantee the printers' bill collectively. For a small publication being produced in a prosperous southern English town by a group, most of whom are employed or retired professional people, it should frankly not be very difficult to raise the sum needed from a group of guarantors. This is much simpler than organising fund-raising events and less demeaning than holding out a begging bowl down at the council offices.

Selling the book once it has appeared should not be too great a struggle if it is reasonably well written and attractively illustrated and printed. Much depends on the community in which you are working. In a pleasant country town with a traditional stock-holding bookshop run by an interested resident proprietor it may be possible for them to act as the main outlet in return for the usual trade terms (35 per cent discount). In the case of bookshops owned by one of the major chains much will depend on a sympathetic branch manager. It is always worth making an occasion of the actual appearance of the book. Hold a public meeting, preferably with a lecture by the author and an exhibition of some kind. Have a large quantity of books on sale at the back of the hall and station the author there to autograph them. Try to get a photograph in the local paper. A well organised evening like this can often shift 25 or 30 per cent of the quantity you have to sell to break even and should stimulate interest which results in further sales in the following weeks.

Your customers, especially libraries and trade agents, have to know where to buy the book. For this reason it is important to print, on the back of the title page, not only the name of the printer (which is a legal requirement) and the date of publication, but also the name of the publisher and the address from which copies can be ordered. An equally important item which should also appear on the same page is the International Standard Book Number for the title. This is a ten-digit figure, embodying elements which identify the country in which the book is published and the name of the publisher, as well as containing a serial number for the title within that publisher's list, which even the smallest publishing enterprise must use if their output is to be handled by the book trade, whose automated systems depend largely on ISBNs. Each publisher is allotted a code by a trade body which manages the scheme in the United Kingdom (ISBN Agency Ltd, 12 Dyott Street, London WC1A 1DF), together with a block of numbers for individual titles, which the publisher then allocates. The small charge for the service is well worth paying, even if you plan to publish only one book, and any individual or group going into self-publishing should contact the Agency well before their first title goes to press, so that they have an ISBN in good time to add to the other standard title page verso information.

A more recent development has been the inclusion of bar-codes on the outside back covers of books (which themselves embody the ISBN among other information). These help with sales through outlets with automated tills and generally add a more professional image to a self-published book. In this case, your printer will obtain the film master for the bar-code from a trade house, once you have allocated an ISBN.

As soon as your book is published, one copy should be sent to the Legal Deposit Office of the British Library (Boston Spa, Wetherby, W. Yorkshire LS23 7BY) and five further copies to the agent who acts for the other national libraries entitled to claim a copy of every book published in Britain (A.T. Smail, 100 Euston Street, London NW1 2HQ). This may seem extravagant but it is the law, and the BL copy will soon repay the investment by generating orders from libraries and booksellers who have seen the details listed in *British National Bibliography*, a comprehensive list compiled from accessions at the library. It is always worth sending a review copy to the local newspaper and to the county local history magazine. Both *The Local Historian* and *Local History Magazine* have sections listing new publications and also publish reviews of a rather smaller number of books. It is therefore worth sending copies to these journals as well, since this may attract orders from ex-residents of an area interested in its history or, in the case of publications on a particular aspect of a community's history, those looking for local studies of that subject, irrespective of which part of the country they come from.

The suggestions made so far in this chapter, aimed mainly at groups who have produced a fairly substantial town or village history, possibly with different people writing different chapters, apply also to those who are merely aiming to publish a booklet, or series of booklets, on aspects of the history of their community. This is in fact often the best way of proceeding. Writing the *History of Barchester* in 256 handsome pages takes a long time; getting it published may involve a great deal of effort and money. Enthusiasm wanes over the years, people leave the area, dissension disrupts the group. Nothing gets published in the end. The same may apply to a group which sets up a local journal as a vehicle for members' research. The first issue of the *Barchester Historian* may be a great success but if the sympathetic print shop manager who did all the typesetting and page make-up at cost price has gone out of business, or if the group's editor and treasurer both move to jobs in another part of the country, the second issue may be a year late. The third may have very few contributions because interest has slackened, and there may never be a fourth. On the other hand, if the Barchester Local History Study Group succeeds in publishing a 48-page, well printed, card-covered booklet on *Barchester in 1851* after a couple of years' work, and sells 500 copies at £4.95 a time, it has (a) achieved something tangible, (b) brought a piece of work to a satisfactory conclusion (c) made some money for the future, and (d) not committed itself to more expenditure on a regular publication. There may then be sufficient enthusiasm to carry on with work for Barchester Papers No 2, on *Roman Barchester*, and another fairly modest publication can be organised.

Working in this way is often the best plan for a new group, especially in a community on whose history little has been written in modern times. Members can see something in print fairly quickly as the result of their efforts, without having to raise large sums, and each of the active researchers can get on with their pet project without interference from others. If someone finishes a good, self-contained essay on *Barchester Inns* it can be published as it stands, rather than put on the side for years as a chapter in a town history or rejected for the *Barchester Historian* because it would fill the entire magazine. If enthusiasm temporarily flags, or funds run low for a couple of years, a series such as this can be suspended without difficulty, whereas subscribers to a magazine become restive if they do not receive something each year for their money. There have been many highly successful groups over the last twenty or thirty years publishing in this way, free from the constraints of filling an annual periodical which rapidly becomes a chore for the editor and a nightmare for the treasurer. Their Research Papers, Occasional Papers or whatever have together made a far greater contribution to the history of local communities than most of the monographs claiming to trace the history of a town from the earliest times to 1914, within the covers of one usually very tedious hardback book.

Below the level of a fairly substantial booklet there is a whole undergrowth of local history publishing undertaken by societies or individuals. Probably the most popular format is the ubiquitous 'trail', a folded single sheet or small pamphlet providing an itinerary around a town or village. Hundreds of these have been published, although few people can claim actually to have seen someone following one of their trails. The attraction of this sort of publication for a newly established group is that it requires virtually no outlay to produce and will usually be sold by any reasonably sympathetic retailer, who will admit that people do occasionally come into their shop prepared to go up to £1.50 for a publication of local interest. Again it serves to enhance members' interest, and that of others, in a local history group that has not been going long enough to think of publishing anything more ambitious. It is particularly important that a trail, or anything similar, be well printed and attractively illustrated, so that it catches attention on a bookstall. As with most other local history publishing, there is now so much material of this kind being produced that the prospective publisher should be able to find several examples available locally as a guide to what constitutes a saleable piece of work.

The view of the local book trade, or its nearest equivalent, on marketing is often worth consulting before any publication is undertaken. Both commercial booksellers and those in charge of sales at museums and heritage centres have a well-honed rule of thumb as to what will sell in their shop. This will be based partly on appearance (people like 'proper books', with nicely set type), partly on format (people do not like A4 pamphlets because they don't fit on bookshelves), but mainly on price. You will be told, *ex cathedra*, that people (often 'people round here' or worse still, 'ordinary people', local historians being somehow extraordinary) will spend £2.50 on a card-covered booklet with a nice picture on the front, will perhaps go to £3.50 if the booklet has the name of their village in the title, but will not pay more than £4.95 under any circumstances. Local history groups have often proved these predictions wrong by publishing hugely successful hardback books at £15 or £20 a time, and certainly books of old photographs at around £10 usually break out of this mould, but for the newly established group deciding how best to publish their first research paper, the advice is worth heeding.

This introduction to self-publishing may seem irrelevant to the needs of the individual amateur beginning research, but it has been included because many local historians soon find themselves involved in group projects and seek advice on publication. Working within a group is probably better than becoming a one-person publisher in any case, partly because it pools expertise and spreads both the work and the financial risk. The group as a whole can discuss the best way of proceeding, taking into account local circumstances, how much money is available, and what members want to do. Self-publishing by a local group, whether through a pamphlet series or a magazine, is how most local historians first see their work in print, and the advice in this chapter may help both with the mechanics of writing local history in a simple but reasonably scholarly way, and in getting it published in an equally simple but nonetheless permanent and attractive form.

Further Reading

The following list is arranged in broadly the same way as the text, with general works followed by those on more specialised topics. I have tried to confine the list to titles which should be available in most public libraries with a local studies section, and references given in these books should provide leads to articles in a variety of scholarly journals or to major reference works for which the resources of a city or university library will be needed. I have not included articles in *The Local Historian* or *Local History Magazine*, although recent issues of both are worth scanning for items of general interest, as well as news and reviews, and again most public libraries subscribe to both titles.

To save space, no title has been listed more than once, although some of the more general books contain material relating to several topics discussed in different chapters here.

For further reading on topics for which nothing is listed here the general works with the most references are W.B. Stephens, Sources for *English Local History* (3rd ed., 1994), my own *Record Sources for Local History* (1987), and *The Oxford Companion to Local and Family History* (ed. David Hey) (1996). There is no general bibliography of works on local history, although there are sections on local works in the standard general bibliographies of English history which will be found in most reference libraries.

The abbreviation 'BALH' indicates a booklet issued by the British Association for Local History, 'FFHS' means the Federation of Family History Societies, and 'PRO' refers to a Public Record Office title.

Chapter 1: Local History Yesterday and Today

On the modern development of the subject the following (listed in order of publication) may be of interest, although only the more recent can be described as still being of value as practical manuals, as opposed to those worth reading for their authors' ideas on what constitutes local history and how it was studied at the time they were writing.

J.C. Cox, *How to write the history of a parish* (Bemrose, 1879 and later eds.).

R.B. Pugh, *How to write a parish history* (Allen & Unwin, 1954).

W.G. Hoskins, *Local history in England* (Longman, 1959; 2nd ed. 1972; 3rd ed. 1984).

W.G. Hoskins, *Provincial England* (Macmillan, 1963).

W.G. Hoskins, *English local history. The past and the future* (Leicester University Press, 1966).

F.G. Emmison, *Archives and local history* (Methuen, 1966).

H.P.R. Finberg and V.H.T. Skipp, Local history. *Objective and pursuit* (David & Charles, 1967).

R. Douch, *Local history and the teacher* (Routledge, 1967).

W.B. Stephens, *Sources for English local history* (1973; 3rd ed. Cambridge University Press, 1981; repr. Phillimore, 1994).

D. Iredale, *Local history research and writing. A manual for local history writers* (Elmfield Press, 1974).

A. Rogers, *Approaches to local history* (Longman, 1977).

W.B. Stephens, *Teaching local history* (Manchester University Press, 1977).

A. Rogers (ed.), *Group projects in local history* (Dawson, 1977).

A. Macfarlane with S. Harrison and C. Jardine, *Reconstructing historical communities* (Cambridge University Press, 1977).

R.W. Dunning, *Local history for beginners* (Phillimore, 1980).

J.R. Ravensdale (ed. B. Brooks), *History on your doorstep* (BBC, 1982).

J. Ravensdale and S. Purkis, *The local history kit* (National Extension College, n.d.; *c.* 1982?).

D. Hey, *Family history and local history in England* (Longman, 1987).

C. Phythian-Adams, *Re-thinking English local history* (Leicester University Press, 1987).

C. Lewis, *Particular places. An introduction to English local history* (British Library, 1989).

C.D. Rogers and J.H. Smith, *Local family history in England 1538-1914* (Manchester University Press, 1991).

K. Tiller, *English local history. An introduction* (Sutton, 1992).

Various editors, *Studying family and community history. 19th and 20th centuries* (Cambridge University Press and Open University, 1994).

M.A. Williams, *Researching local history: the human journey* (Longman, 1996).

J. Griffin and T. Lomas, *Exploring local history* (Teach Yourself Books, 1997).

There have been several attempts at encylopaedic reference books for local historians, of which those by David Hey are the most useful:

D. Hey, *The Oxford guide to family history* (Oxford University Press, 1993).
D. Hey (ed.), *The Oxford companion to local and family history* (Oxford University Press, 1996).
D. Hey, *The Oxford dictionary of local and family history* (Oxford University Press, 1997).
J. Campbell-Kease, *A companion to local history research* (A. & C. Black, 1989).
J. Richardson, *The local historian's encyclopaedia* (Historical Publications, 2nd ed. 1993).

General works on antiquarianism include:

D.C. Douglas, *English scholars* (Cape, 1951).
L. Fox (ed.), *English historical scholarship in the sixteenth and seventeenth centuries* (Dugdale Society, 1956).
F.S. Fussner, *The historical revolution. English historical writing and thought, 1580-1640* (Routledge, 1962).
E.A.L. Moir, *The discovery of Britain. The English tourists, 1540-1840* (Routledge, 1964).
R.B. Pugh (ed.), *Victoria History of the Counties of England. General introduction* (Oxford University Press, 1970).
C.R. Elrington (ed.), *Victoria History of the Counties of England. General introduction: supplement 1970-90* (Oxford University Press, 1990).
J. Simmons (ed.), *English county historians* (EP, 1978).
T.D. Kendrick, *British antiquity* (Methuen, 2nd ed. 1970).
P. Levine, *The amateur and the professional. Antiquarians, historians and archaeologists in Victorian England, 1838-1886* (Cambridge University Press, 1986).

S.A.E. Mendyk, *'Speculum Britanniae'. Regional study, antiquarianism, and science in Britain to 1700* (University of Toronto Press, 1989).

C.R.J. Currie and C.P. Lewis (ed.), *English county histories. A guide* (Sutton, 1994).

Chapter 2: At the Library

Most local studies libraries issue brief guides to their collection as a whole and to particular topics. Larger reference libraries should also have the main reference books on the sources discussed in this chapter.

S. Guy, *English local studies handbook. A guide to resources for each county including libraries, record offices, societies, journals and museums* (University of Exeter Press, 1992). Superseded for record offices by the HMC title listed under Chapter 3, but still useful for other addresses. A new edition is in preparation.

J.L. Hobbs, *Local history and the library* (Deutsch, 1962).

R. Harvey, *Genealogy for librarians* (Clive Bingley, 1983).

J.E. Norton, *Guide to national and provincial directories of England and Wales, excluding London, published before 1856* (Royal Historical Society, 1950).

C.W.F. Goss, *The London directories, 1677-1855* (Archer, 1932).

G. Shaw and A. Tipper, *British directories: a bibliography and guide to directories published in England and Wales (1850-1950) and Scotland (1773-1950)* (Leicester University Press, 1988).

British Library, *Catalogue of the Newspaper Library* (BL, 1975).

The Times tercentenary handlist of English and Welsh newspapers, magazines and reviews, 1620-1920 (The Times, 1920).

J.S.W. Gibson, *Local newspapers, 1750-1920: England and Wales, Channel Islands, Isle of Man. A select location list* (FFHS, new ed. in preparation).

M. Murphy, *Newspapers and local history* (BALH, 1991).

E.L.C. Mullins (ed.), *A guide to the historical and archaeological publications of societies in England and Wales, 1901-33* (Royal Historical Society, 1958).

E.L.C. Mullins (ed.), *Texts and calendars. An analytical guide to serial publications* (Royal Historical Society, 1968).

E.L.C. Mullins (ed.), *Texts and calendars II. An analytical guide to serial publications, 1957-1982* (Royal Historical Society, 1983).
M.W. Barley, *A guide to British topographical collections* (Council for British Archaeology, 1974).
G. Oliver, *Photographs and local history* (Batsford, 1989).

There are several useful guides to the census and its records:

J.S.W. Gibson and E. Hampson, *Census Returns 1841-1891 In microform. A directory to local holdings in Great Britain, Channel Islands, Isle of Man* (FFHS, 1996).
J.S.W. Gibson, *Local census listings, 1522-1930. Holdings in the British Isles* (FFHS, 1997).
J.S.W. Gibson and C. Chapman, *Marriage, census and other indexes for family historians* (FFHS, 1996).
Office of Population Censuses and Surveys, *Guide to Census Reports, 1801-1966* (HMSO, 1977).
E.A. Wrigley (ed.), *Nineteenth-century society. Essays in the use of quantitative methods for the study of social data* (Cambridge University Press, 1972).
R. Lawton (ed.), *The census and social structure. An interpretive guide to the nineteenth-century Censuses for England and Wales* (Cass, 1978).
E. Higgs, *Making sense of the census. The manuscript returns for England and Wales, 1801-1901* (HMSO, 1989).
E. Higgs, *A clearer sense of the census* (Stationery Office, 1995).
S. Lumas, *Making use of the census* (PRO, 1997).

Chapter 3: At the Record Office

On record offices themselves and general problems of using archives, such as palaeography, chronology and Latin, see the following:

J.S.W. Gibson and P. Peskett, *Record offices: how to find them* (FFHS 1996).
Historical Manuscripts Commission, *Record repositories in Great Britain* (PRO, 1997).

A. Ison, *The secretary hand ABC* (Berkshire Books, 1994).

F.G. Emmison, *How to read local archives*, 1550-1700 (Historical Association, 1967).

L. Munby, *Reading Tudor and Stuart handwriting* (BALH, 1988).

L.C Hector, *The handwriting of English documents* (Kohler & Coombes, 1980).

E. Danbury, *Palaeography for historians* (Phillimore, 1998).

K.C. Newton, *Medieval local records. A reading aid* (Historical Association, 1971).

C.T. Martin, *The record interpreter* (Phillimore, 1994).

C.R. Cheney (ed.), *Handbook of dates for students of English history* (Royal Historical Society, 1970).

F.M. Powicke and E.B. Fryde, *Handbook of British chronology* (Royal Historical Society, 1971).

E.A. Gooder, *Latin for local history. An introduction* (Longman, 1978).

D. Stuart, *Latin for local and family historians* (Phillimore, 1995).

R.E. Latham (ed.), *Revised medieval Latin word list* (Oxford University Press, 1965).

J. Bristow, *The local historian's glossary and* vade mecum (University of Nottingham, Dept of Adult Education, 1990).

Numerous books and pamphlets provide guides to the records of local administration, the church, landownership and the other subjects mentioned in this chapter:

J. West, *Village records* (1962; 3rd ed. Phillimore, 1997).

J. West, *Town records* (Phillimore, 1983).

F.G. Emmison, *Introduction to archives* (Phillimore, 1977).

D. Iredale, *Enjoying archives* (Phillimore, 1985).

C Kitching, *Archives. The very essence of our heritage* (Phillimore, 1996).

L.M. Munby (ed.), *Short guides to records* (Historical Association, 1972).

C.D. Rogers, *The family tree detective. A manual for analysing and solving genealogical problems in England and Wales, 1538 to the present day* (Manchester University Press, 1983).

C.D. Rogers, *Tracing missing persons. An introduction to agencies, methods and sources in England and Wales* (Manchester University Press, 1986).

W.E. Tate, *The parish chest* (3rd ed., Phillimore, 1983).

B. Keith-Lucas, *English local government in the nineteenth and twentieth centuries* (Historical Association, 1977).

F.G. Emmison and I. Gray, *County records (Quarter Sessions, Petty Sessions, Clerk of the Peace and Lieutenancy)* (Historical Association, 1973).

J.S.W. Gibson, *Quarter sessions records for family historians. A select list* (FFHS, 1995).

P. Riden, *How to trace the history of your car* (2nd ed., Merton Priory Press, 1998).

J.S.W. Gibson and D.R. Mills, *Land tax assessments, c. 1690–c. 1950* (FFHS, 1983).

M. Turner and D. Mills (ed.), *Land and property: the English land tax 1692-1832* (Alan Sutton, 1986).

J.S.W. Gibson and J. Hunter, *Victuallers' licences* (FFHS, 1997).

J.S.W. Gibson, *Poll books, c. 1696-1872. A directory to holdings in Great Britain* (FFHS, 1994).

J.S.W. Gibson, *Electoral registers since 1832, and burgess rolls* (FFHS, 1990).

J.S.W. Gibson and C. Rogers, *Poor law union records* (set of four regional volumes and gazetteer of England and Wales) (FFHS, 1997).

J.S.W. Gibson, *Coroners' records in England and Wales* (FFHS, 1997).

J.S.W. Gibson and M. Medlycott, *Militia lists and musters, 1757-1856* (FFHS, 1994).

J.S.W. Gibson and D. Mills, Land and window tax assessments (FFHS, 1997).

P.D.A. Harvey, *Manorial records* (British Records Association, 1984).

M. Ellis, *Using manorial records* (PRO, 1997).

D. Stuart, *Manorial records* (Phillimore, 1992).

P. Bushell, *Tracing the history of your house* (Pavilion, 1989).

J.H. Harvey, *Sources for the history of a house* (British Records Association, 1974).

B. Greysmith, *Tracing the history of your house* (Hodder & Stoughton, 1994).

A.A. Dibben, *Title deeds 13th-19th centuries* (Historical Association, 1971).

N.W. Alcock, *Old title deeds. A guide for local and family historians* (Phillimore, 1994).

D.J. Steel (ed.), *National index of parish registers* (Society of Genealogists, 1968-).

M. Nissel, *People count. A history of the General Register Office* (HMSO, 1987).

C.R. Humphery-Smith, *The Phillimore atlas and index of parish registers* (Phillimore, 1995).

D.M. Owen, *The records of the established church in England, excluding parochial records* (British Records Association, 1970).

A. Tarver, *Church court records* (Phillimore, 1995).

J.S.W. Gibson, *Bishops' transcripts and marriage licences. A guide to their location and indexes* (FFHS, 1997).

M. Walcot and J.S.W. Gibson, *Marriage indexes. How to find them, how to use them, how to compile one* (FFHS, 1980).

A.J. Camp, *Wills and their whereabouts* (Society of Genealogists, 1974).

J.S.W. Gibson, *Wills and where to find them* (Phillimore, 1974).

J.S.W. Gibson, *A simplified guide to probate jurisdiction. Where to look for wills* (FFHS, 1980).

A.J. Camp (ed.), *An index to the wills proved in the Prerogative Court of Canterbury, 1750-1800* (Society of Genealogists, 1976-92).

M. Scott, *Prerogative Court of Canterbury wills and other probate records* (PRO, 1997).

J. Cox, *The records of the Prerogative Court of Canterbury and the Death Duty Registers* (PRO, 1980).

R. Milward, *A glossary of household, farming and trade terms from probate inventories* (Derbyshire Record Society, 1982).

Burke's Peerage, *Burke's family index* (Burke's Peerage, 1976).

E.A. Wrigley, *An introduction to English historical demography from the sixteenth to nineteenth century* (Weidenfeld & Nicolson, 1966).

M. Mullett, *Sources for the history of English Nonconformity 1660-1830* (British Records Association, 1991).

D. Shaney, *Protestant Nonconformity and Roman Catholicism* (PRO, 1996).

T.C. Barker and others, *Business history* (Historical Association, 1960).

J. Orbell, *A guide to tracing the history of a business* (Gower, 1987).

Records of British business and industry 1760-1914. Metal processing and engineering (HMSO, 1994).

Chapter 4: Maps

In addition to many local map bibliographies, either published or kept on cards in a library or record office, there are several very useful general references in this field:

J.B. Harley, *Maps for the local historian. A guide to British sources* (BALH, 1972).

J.B. Harley and C.W. Phillips, *The historian's guide to Ordnance Survey maps* (BALH, 1965).

C. Close, *The early years of the Ordnance Survey* (Repr. David & Charles, 1969).

W.A. Seymour (ed.), *A history of the Ordnance Survey* (Dawson, 1980).

E.J. Evans, *Tithes. Maps, apportionments and the 1836 Act* (BALH, 1993).

R.J.P. Kain and H.C. Prince, *The tithe surveys of England and Wales* (Cambridge University Press, 1985).

E.M. Rodger, *The large scale county maps of the British Isles, 1596 1850. A union list* (Bodleian Library, 1972).

British Museum, *Catalogue of printed maps, charts and plans to 1964* (BM, 1967).

Maps and plans in the Public Record Office. I. British Isles c. 1410 1860 (HMSO, 1967).

B.P. Hindle, *Maps for local history* (Batsford, 1988).

D. Smith, *Maps and plans for the local historian and collector* (Batsford, 1988).

R. Oliver, *Ordnance Survey maps. A concise guide for historians* (Charles Close Society, 1991).

W. Foot, *Maps for family history* (PRO, 1994).

With maps may conveniently be coupled place-names:

E. Ekwall, *Concise Oxford dictionary of English place-names* (Oxford University Press, 4th ed. 1960).

A.H. Smith, *English place-name elements* (English Place-Name Society, 1956).

K. Cameron, *English place-names* (Batsford, 1977).

M. Gelling, *Signposts to the past* (Phillimore, 1988).

P.H. Reaney, *The origin of English place-names* (Routledge, 1960).

J. Field, *English field-names. A dictionary* (David & Charles, 1972).

I.H. Adams, *Agrarian landscape terms. A glossary for historical geography* (Institute of British Geographers, 1976).

Ordnance Survey, *Place names on maps of Scotland and Wales. A glossary of the most common Gaelic and Scandinavian elements used on maps of Scotland and of the most common Welsh elements used on maps of Wales* (OS, 1973).

Chapter 5: Landscapes and Buildings

There is a very large literature on the subjects covered by this chapter. General books on fieldwork in local history, landscape history and the relationship between history and archaeology include:

W.G. Hoskins, *The making of the English landscape* (Hodder & Stoughton, 1955).

M.W. Beresford, *History on the ground* (Methuen, 1971).

W.G. Hoskins, *Fieldwork in local history* (Faber, 1967).

D.P. Dymond, *Archaeology for the historian* (Historical Association, 1967).

A. Rogers and T. Rowley (ed.), *Landscapes and documents* (BALH, 1974).

D.P. Dymond, *Archaeology and history. A plea for reconciliation* (Thames & Hudson, 1974).

C.C. Taylor, *Fieldwork in medieval archaeology* (Batsford, 1974).

C. Platt, *Medieval archaeology in England. A guide to the historical sources* (Pinhorn, 1969).

M. Aston, *Interpreting the landscape. Landscape archaeology in local studies* (Batsford, 1985).

O. Rackham, *The history of the countryside* (Dent, 1986).

More specifically on the medieval and post-medieval landscape:

M.W. Beresford and J.K. St Joseph, *Medieval England. An aerial survey* (Cambridge University Press, 1958; 2nd ed. 1979).

M.W. Beresford and J.G. Hurst (ed.), *Deserted medieval villages. Studies* (Lutterworth Press, 1971).

M.D. Hooper and others, *Hedges and local history* (BALH, 1971).

A.R.H. Butler and R.A. Butlin (ed.), *Studies of field systems in the British Isles* (Cambridge University Press, 1973).

R.C. Russell, *The logic of open field systems* (BALH, 1975).

C.C. Taylor, *Fields in the English landscape* (Dent, 1975).

P.H. Sawyer (ed.), *Medieval settlement. Continuity and change* (Edward Arnold, 1976).

D. Crossley, *Post-medieval archaeology in Britain* (Leicester University Press, 1990).

A. Brown, *Fieldwork for archaeologists and local historians* (Batsford, 1987).

Some works on industrial archaeology of permanent interest:

M.M. Rix, *Industrial archaeology* (Historical Association, 1967).

R.A. Buchanan, *Industrial archaeology in Britain* (Penguin, 1972).

N. Cossons, *The BP book of industrial archaeology* (David & Charles, 3rd ed. 1993).

J.K. Major, *Fieldwork in industrial archaeology* (Batsford, 1975).

J.P.M. Pannell, *The techniques of industrial archaeology* (David & Charles, 2nd ed. 1974).

K. Falconer, *Guide to England's industrial heritage* (Batsford, 1980).

B. Trinder, *The making of the industrial landscape* (Dent, 1982).

B. Trinder, *The Blackwell encyclopaedia of industrial archaeology* (Blackwell, 1992).

M. Stratton and B. Trinder, *English Heritage book of industrial England* (Batsford, 1997).

On vernacular architecture:

M.W. Barley, *The English farm house and cottage* (Routledge, 1961).

M.E. Wood, *The English medieval house* (Phoenix House, 1965).

P.M.G. Eden, *Small houses in England, 1520-1820. Towards a classification* (Historical Association, 1969).

R.W. Brunskill, *Illustrated handbook of vernacular architecture* (Faber, 1970).

R.W. Brunskill, *Traditional buildings of England: an introduction to vernacular architecture* (Gollancz, 1992).

R.W. Brunskill, *Houses and cottages of Britain. Origins and development of traditional buildings* (Gollancz, 1997).

V. Parker, *The English house in the nineteenth century* (Historical Association, 1970).

N. Harvey, *A history of farm buildings in England and Wales* (David & Charles, 1970).

A. Clifton-Taylor, *The pattern of English building* (Faber, 1972).

P. Addyman and M.K. Morris (ed.), *The archaeological study of churches* (Council for British Archaeology, 1976).

J. and J. Penoyre, *Houses in the landscape. A regional study of vernacular building styles in England and Wales* (Faber, 1978).

E. Mercer, *English vernacular houses* (HMSO, 1975).

T. Buchanan, *Photographing historic buildings for the record* (HMSO, 1983).

P. Swallow, D. Watt and R. Ashton, *Measurement and recording of historic buildings* (Donhead Publishing, 1993).

Chapter 6: The PRO and other National Collections

All the institutions mentioned in this chapter issue leaflets outlining their collections and arrangements for readers. The guides listed here should be available in most public libraries. It is worth noting that since being freed from publishing through HMSO, the PRO has greatly expanded its range of titles for local and family history.

J.D. Cantwell, *The Public Record Office 1838-1958* (HMSO, 1991).

A. Lawes, *Chancery Lane 1377-1977* (PRO, 1996).

Guide to the contents of the Public Record Office (HMSO, 1963-8).

Guide to the Public Record Office (PRO, 1999). Available only on microfiche.

J. Cox, *New to Kew?* (PRO, 1997).

J. Cox and S. Colwell, *Never been here before?* (PRO, 1997). An introduction to the Family Records Centre, similar to Mrs Cox's guide to the PRO itself cited above.

J. Cox and T. Padfield, *Tracing your ancestors in the Public Record Office* (PRO, 1998).

P. Riden, *Record sources for local history* (Batsford, 1987).

M. Jurkowski, C. Smith and D. Crook, *Lay taxes in England and Wales 1188-1688* (PRO, 1998).

H. Horwitz, *Chancery and Equity records and proceedings 1600-1800* (PRO, 1998).

R.W. Hoyle, *Tudor taxation records* (PRO, 1994).

J.S.W. Gibson, *The hearth tax, other later Stuart tax lists and the Association Oath rolls* (FFHS, 1996).

K. Schurer and T. Arkell (ed.), *Surveying the people. The interpretation and use of document sources for the study of population in the later seventeenth century* (Leopard's Head Press, 1992).

J.S.W. Gibson and A. Dell, *Tudor and Stuart muster rolls* (FFHS, 1989).

J.S.W. Gibson, *The Protestation Returns 1641–42 and other contemporary listings* (FFHS, 1995).

A. Morton, *Education and the state from 1833* (PRO, 1997).

A. Morton and G. Donaldson, *British national archives and the local historian. A guide to official record publications* (Historical Association, 1980).

M.A.E. Nickson, *The British Library. Guide to the catalogues and indexes of the Department of Manuscripts* (BL, 1978).

A.R. Wagner, *The records and collections of the College of Arms* (Burke's Peerage, 1974).

M.P. Bond, *Guide to the records of Parliament* (HMSO, 1971).

National Library of Wales, *Guide to the Department of Manuscripts and Records* (NLW, 1994).

Introductory works on parliamentary papers include:

W.R. Powell, *Local history from Blue Books. A select list of the sessional papers of the House of Commons* (Historical Association, 1962).

P. and G. Ford, *Select list of British parliamentary papers, 1833-99* (Irish Universities Press, 1969).

P. and G. Ford, *Guide to parliamentary papers: what they are, how to find them, how to use them* (Irish Universities Press, 1972).

Chapter 7: Writing and Publication

This chapter is based largely on my own experience in local history publishing and there is no full-scale guide to the subject. The following may help those venturing in this direction.

D. Dymond, *Writing local history* (BALH, 1996).

A.G. Hodgkiss, *Maps for books and theses* (David & Charles, 1970). Out of date in its discussion of materials and technical aids, but the basic advice remains sound.

D. Dymond, *Writing a church guide* (Church Information Office and BALH, 1977).

R. McLean, *The Thames and Hudson manual of typography* (Thames & Hudson, 1980). A much better introduction for the non-specialist than the typical book on 'layout for desktop publishing' sold in computer stores.

R.F. Hunnisett, *Editing records for publication* (British Records Association, 1977).

R.F. Hunnisett, *Indexing for editors* (British Records Association, 1972). Useful for those indexing books other than record texts who want to do it properly.

Index

abstracts of title 66
accounting records 77-8
Acts of Parliament 155-7
Additional Manuscripts, at British Library 152
administration of intestate estates 70-3
admons 70-3
adult education and local history 2, 3, 16-17, 19
advowsons 94
air photographs 124
alehouse recognisances 79
Amateur Historian, The: see Local Historian, The
Ancient Deeds, at PRO 146
ancient monuments 127-8
Ancient Monuments Commissions: *see* Royal Commissions on Ancient Monuments
Anglo-Saxon archaeology 111-12
    estate boundaries 124
antiquarian collections 34-5, 153, 155
Antiquaries, Society of 11
apportionments, tithe 95
Archaeologia 11
archaeology, field 111-14
    history of 11-13
    organisation of 119-20
    value for local history 115-19
    see also industrial archaeology; medieval archaeology; post-medieval archaeology; rescue archaeology
archdeacons, probate jurisdiction of 70
architectural history
    and local history 125-32
    modern developments in 112
    see also vernacular architecture
archival references, how to present 165-7
archive services: *see* county record offices, Public Record Office
Assize courts 74-5
Association for Industrial Archaeology 18, 114

Augmentations, Court of, records 145-6
author-date (Harvard) system of references 167
awards, tithe 95

baptism, registration of 72-3
bar-codes, on book covers 173
bargain and sale, deeds of 62-3
Barnsley (Yorks.) 132
baron, manor court 64-5
basket weaving, history of 27
bibliographical references, how to present 24-5, 27-8, 165-7
bills, Parliamentary 155-7
Birmingham (Warwicks.) 132
    City Library 20-1, 41
birth, registration of 72-3, 150
bishops, probate jurisdiction of 70
bishop's transcripts of parish registers 69
Blue Books 156
BM: *see* British Library
board schools 55-6
boards of guardians 54-5, 57
Bodleian Library, Oxford 34, 85, 155
bonds, administration 72
book design, importance of in self-publishing 171
book trade, hints on dealing with 172, 174-5
booklets, often better than books as outlet for research 173-4
books of reference (with deposited plans) 107
boroughs
    medieval 100-1
    municipal and county 57-9
    records 148
Borthwick Institute of Historical Research, York 70, 157
boundaries
    estate and manor 93
    parish 93, 96
    township 93

Bray, William 11
bridges, history of 80
bridle-paths, and inclosure awards 106
Bristol 43
British Association for Local History 7,
    18
British Coal 78
British Library 85-6, 91
    Department of Manuscripts 34, 151-4
    Legal Deposit Office 173
    Map Room 88
British Museum: *see* British Library
British National Bibliography 173
British Rail/Railways 81
British Steel Corporation 78-9
British Transport Commission 80
British Waterways Museum 80
Brunskill, R.W. 126
building leases 63
buildings, as evidence for local history
    125-32
Buildings of England/of Wales series 127
Burford (Oxon.) 131-2
burial, registration of 72-3
Burton, William 10
business history, sources for 73-4, 76-9,
    147
bye-law housing 129

Cadw: Welsh Historic Monuments 125,
    127-8
calendar, changes in the 65
    of records 48
Cambrian Archaeological Association 13
Cambridge University Library 85, 155
Camden, William 11-12
camera-ready copy 170
canals, sources for history of 80, 96,
    106-7, 155-6
Canterbury, Prerogative Court of 70-3
card indexes, and local history 24
CARN tickets 46
carrying services, history of 29, 79
cartularies 151
Catalogue of Ancient Deeds, at PRO 146
Catholic records 158
census enumerators' books 35-9, 61, 69,
    101-2, 150
Centre for Kentish Studies 157
Chancery, records of 145, 148
chantries, history of 145-6
Charles Close Society 89

charters, borough 58, 59
    medieval 151-2
Chester, Palatinate of 145
Chesterfield (Derbys.) 132
Church Commissioners 157
Church of England records 42-3, 157
    see also parish records
Church of England Records Centre 157
church rates 53
    schools 55-6
Church in Wales, records of 158-9
churchwardens 52-3
civil marriage 73
    parishes 50-1
        see also parishes
    wills 72
co-partnership, deeds of 77
coach services, history of 29, 79
Coal Authority 78
coal industry, history of 76, 78
College of Arms 153-4
college records, Oxford and Cambridge
    155
common fields, inclosure of 103-5
communities, in Wales 50
Companies House, records 77, 147
company history 76-9, 147
computers and local history 24
constables, high and petty 52-3
conveyances 62-3
copyhold tenure 65
Copyright, Crown, and Ordnance Survey
    maps 87-8
Copyright libraries, legal requirements
    173
Cornwall, Duchy of 60, 145
council houses 57, 130
councils: *see* boroughs, county, parish,
    rural district and urban district
    councils
counties, metropolitan 59
county antiquarian journals 16, 22, 162-3
    societies 12-13, 16, 19,26
County Archive Research Network 46
county bridges 80
    borough councils 57-9
    councils 57-9, 79-80
    directories 29-31
    histories 8-14, 22, 28
        see also Victoria History of the
        Counties of England
    maps 90-1